THINKING
in the
CLASSROOM
A Survey of Programs

THINKING
in the
CLASSROOM
A Survey of Programs

PAUL CHANCE
Chesapeake College

Foreword by
Ronald S. Brandt

Teachers College, Columbia University
New York and London

Published by Teachers College Press, 1234 Amsterdam Avenue, New York, N.Y. 10027

The preparation of this volume was supported in part by a grant from the National Institute of Education (Grant NIE-G-78-0215). The volume is based in part on papers presented at a National Institute of Education-sponsored conference on thinking and learning held at the Learning Research and Development Center, University of Pittsburgh, Pittsburgh, PA. The points of view and opinions expressed in the volume are entirely the author's, and no endorsement by the National Institute of Education or the University of Pittsburgh is implied.

Library of Congress Cataloging in Publication Data

Chance, Paul.
     Thinking in the classroom.

     Bibliography: p.
     Includes index.
     1. Creative thinking (Education)   2. Thought
and thinking—Study and teaching.   3.   Problem
solving—Study and teaching.   I.   Title.
LB1062.C48   1985   370.15'7   85-17335

ISBN 0–8077–2794–6

Manufactured in the United States of America

91 90 89 88 87 86   2 3 4 5 6

For
David R. Stone

Contents

Foreword

One reason for the growing interest in teaching thinking is the many programs designed specifically for that purpose. These programs differ in many ways: in their theoretical rationale, in their methods, in the type of students for whom they are intended, in the kinds of thinking they teach, and in the evidence of their effectiveness. Most do not fall into neat categories, and "figuring them out" is often difficult. Yet many of the programs apparently achieve remarkable results and cannot be ignored.

Thus educators and their allies have some tough decisions to make. In deciding which, if any, programs to select, curriculum specialists, school administrators, principals, teachers, and parents ideally should

- Examine the programs and their supporting materials
- Talk with the program developers or their representatives
- Meet with teachers and others who have used the materials
- Observe the programs in use
- Read research reports on their effectiveness

In reality, few educators have the time to conduct such a thorough investigation. That is where Paul Chance's book comes in, for he has done much of this work for the reader. He has set forth the kinds of information people would hope to acquire on their own, and he has done so in a clear and elegant style that is a pleasure to read.

This isn't to say that *Thinking in the Classroom* will make the choice of a program easy. Those involved in the decision-making process will still have much to consider. But by explaining so clearly the assumptions, goals, methods, materials, audience, teacher qualifications, benefits, and problems of each program, Paul Chance gives us a leg up on the decision process. Even the reader who eventually rejects all the approaches reviewed here will find that he or she has learned much that will help in exploring other possibilities. Indeed, one thing the book makes plain is that these programs have much to teach us.

RONALD S. BRANDT

Acknowledgments

Many people contributed to this book. Without the financial support of the National Institute of Education, its writing would not have been possible. Several people at N.I.E. read a draft of the book and made many useful comments; I am particularly grateful to Judith Segal for her advice, patience, and moral support. Robert Glaser, Director of the Learning Research and Development Center, University of Pittsburgh, also read an early version of the book and offered good advice. Ronald Brandt, Executive Editor of *Educational Leadership*, kindly consented to write the Foreword.

I also wish to thank the principal developers of the programs described herein. Each developer not only answered written and oral queries but read and commented upon a draft of the chapter describing his or her respective program. This helped to ensure that the chapters represented the programs in a fair and accurate way. I am glad to offer thanks to Marilyn Adams, Edward deBono, Martin Covington, Donald Dansereau, Reuven Feuerstein, Jack Lochhead, Matthew Lipman, Raymond Nickerson, and Arthur Whimbey.

I am grateful to the following individuals and publishers for generously allowing me to use material from various programs: Charles E. Merrill Publishing Company (Productive Thinking Program), Direct Education Services, Ltd. (CoRT Thinking Lessons), Donald Dansereau (Techniques of Learning), Franklin Institute Press (Problem Solving and Comprehension), Institute for the Advancement of Philosophy for Children (Philosophy for Children), Mastery Education Corporation (Odyssey), and University Park Press and Reuven Feuerstein (Instrumental Enrichment).

In addition, I am indebted to the library staffs of the University of Delaware, the University of Maryland, Salisbury State College, Chesapeake College, and Caroline County. I also wish to thank the expert staff of Teachers College Press: Lois Patton and Carole Saltz each made important contributions to the book; Judy Davis prepared the index; I am especially grateful to Susan Liddicoat and Florence Stickney for their very careful editing of the manuscript.

All these people helped improve this book. However, I alone am responsible for any flaws or shortcomings that may remain.

1 Introduction: The Thinking Movement

Amid the hoopla of the "back to basics" movement, a quieter, yet more profound change has been taking place in American education. While many people are satisfied that what is needed in our schools is more drill in the mechanics of reading, writing, and 'rithmetic, professional educators—the people trained for and charged with the task of educating our children—have increasingly rejected this simplistic idea. Many of them now believe that we must offer our students more than rote drill, more than minimal competencies, more than facts. We must begin to teach our children how to evaluate information, how to apply information, how to produce information. We must teach them, in other words, *how to think*.

In 1984, Ronald Brandt, editor of *Educational Leadership*, wrote that "we are seeing the beginnings of a major new movement to promote intellectual development" (p. 3). The breadth and depth of commitment among educators to this movement is quite remarkable. When, in 1984, the Association for Supervision and Curriculum Development (ASCD), whose members include many of the nation's educational movers and shakers, asked a sample of its members what educational topics they wanted more information on, 82 percent named instruction in thinking.[1] In a 1984 poll (Gallup, 1985), teachers ranked improvement in thinking as the most important of twenty-five educational goals.[2] Workshops, conferences, and lectures in thinking instruction are being offered all over the country and attract overflow crowds. In August 1984, for example, a Harvard University conference on thinking intended for a hundred or so upper-echelon school officials registered six hundred and turned away another twelve hundred. Thousands of teachers are studying methods of teaching thinking, and school superintendents everywhere, it seems, are appointing task forces to develop ways of improving thinking ability. In a decade of shrinking budgets and no-frills education, thinking has become the fastest-growing subject in our schools.[3]

What has given rise to this unprecedented interest in teaching thinking? The answer seems to be the growing realization among educators that our society is in the midst of a profound cultural transformation, one that will produce a world in which high-level thinking is a basic skill.

In his 1980 book, *The Third Wave*, Alvin Toffler identifies three great advances, or waves, in the history of civilization. The first was the development of agriculture ten thousand years ago. It brought with it a shift from an itinerant, hunting and gathering form of life to stable communities and the working and leisure classes. During this agrarian age, formal education was a luxury of the rich. Most people learned to do the work of the farm and little else.

The second wave, the development of reliable and efficient machines, brought with it the industrial age. This period began around the beginning of the eighteenth century. Large numbers of people left the farms and sought work in the factories that were springing up in the cities. During this period, education of the masses became an important goal, not merely in the United States but throughout the industrialized world. Children who had helped their parents on the farm went off to school to be prepared for a lifetime of factory work. They learned a little of the three Rs, but more importantly they learned the kinds of habits so necessary for the work of the assembly line: to be punctual, to follow instructions, to be quiet, to recognize the authority of a supervisor, and to work at monotonous tasks for long periods of time.

The third wave, the development of automation and electronic computers, began around the middle of this century, and is bringing with it the information age. It is an age in which things are built by things, and people work on ideas. Such knowledge workers create, revise, and communicate information. Today they are found chiefly in banking, insurance, government, communications, publishing, computer programming, education, medicine, law, and research, but they are pushing their way into every corner of our society. The third wave is not yet fully upon us, but it is well under way. In 1950, only 17 percent of the work force held information-related jobs, but by 1982 the figure was over 60 percent (Naisbitt, 1982). By the end of the decade perhaps three out of four Americans will earn their pay by manipulating information.

As our society has become more information oriented, our students have spent more time in the classroom. A hundred years ago, only about one out of every ten students who entered the first grade went on to graduate from high school. Today, three out of four graduate, and about half of those go on to college. Does this mean that our industrial-age education is meeting the needs of the information age? No, it does not. Countless studies have demonstrated that while our students are learning the elementary skills that were sufficient for a lifetime of factory work, they are not learning the higher-level skills required for the information age.

Take reading, for instance. Most high school students can read a passage and answer factual questions (Who shot John?), but they have considerably more trouble answering questions that require drawing some sort of inference from the passage (e.g., Falkof and Moss, 1984; NAEP, 1981). They also have a hard time identifying an author's main points, ranking the relevant importance of his ideas, and detecting logical contradictions (e.g., Brown and Smiley, 1977; Markman, in press). The National Assessment of Educational Progress (NAEP, 1981), which regularly tests student achievement in various areas, has concluded that most seventeen-year-olds lack the ability to analyze a story or poem. Asked to do so, most simply rephrase it or make a value judgment about it. According to the NAEP report:

> Students seem satisfied with their initial interpretations of what they have read and seem genuinely puzzled at requests to explain or defend their points of view. As a result, responses to assessment items requiring explanations of criteria, analysis of text or defense of a judgment or point of view were in general disappointing. Few students could provide more than superficial responses to such tasks, and even the "better" responses showed little evidence of well-developed problem solving strategies or critical-thinking skills. (NAEP, 1981, p. 2)

Similarly, our industrial-age education teaches most students the mechanics of spelling, grammar, and punctuation, but does less well at teaching the higher-level skills of writing. When, in 1984, Maryland's ninth graders took a functional writing test, nearly half of them failed (Fletcher, 1984). But the high failure rate was due largely to poor content and organization, not poor mechanics. NAEP has found the same thing on the national level. In one study (NAEP, 1980), 75 percent of the seventeen-year-clds tested were able to write with few mechanical errors, but when asked to write a per-suasive essay requiring analytical thinking, only 15 percent were judged competent.

The same pattern is seen in mathematics. Study after study finds that most students have a very satisfactory grasp of basic arithmetic functions and can solve simple problems when phrased in familiar form. But they get into trouble when they are given a problem that requires that they do more than mechanically apply a memorized formula. For instance, one NAEP (1983) study gave thirteen-year-olds this problem: "An army bus holds 36 soldiers. If 1,128 soldiers are being bussed to their training site, how many busses are needed?" (p. 26). About 70 percent of the students did the necessary division correctly, but almost half of the students either ignored the remainder or gave the exact quotient (31.33) as their answer.

Clearly, most of our students are learning how to perform the mechanical skills of the three Rs, but they are not learning the higher-level skills of thinking. Yet we are entering a period when these thinking skills are increasingly important. The upshot of this is that by 1990 as many as two million high school graduates may lack the thinking skills required for employment in a complex, technological information society (Gisi and Forbes, 1982).

Some people argue that poor student thinking is due to our having abandoned traditional teaching methods.[4] But studies have shown that what goes on in classrooms today is little different from what went on at the turn of the century (see Goodlad, 1983; Sir-otnik, 1981, 1983). Typically, a teacher stands before his students, giving forth on some subject. The students sit at their desks listening or taking notes. Periodically the teacher asks questions. Usually these can be answered in a few words, often by repeating some part of what the teacher has just said. Often a series of questions is asked of several students in rapid succession. Generally questions are assumed to have one (and only one) right answer, and the teacher is the final arbiter on matters of truth. There is little discussion. The purpose of asking questions is not to stimulate thoughtful examination of a topic, but to provide a kind of drill and to keep the students "on their toes." When the teacher has "covered the material," he gives a homework assignment or a class exercise. This usually consists of reading a text and answering a series of questions. These questions usually can be answered in a few words drawn from the text, and many students search the text for answers without having read, let alone thought about, a single page.

Some readers may doubt that the image of school just depicted is still accurate today, so it may be useful to review some recent research findings. Studies have found, for example, that after the first two grades, instruction in reading can be characterized as "assign and test." In one study (Durkin, 1978), less than 1 percent of reading instruction involved teaching students how to understand written material. Usually teachers told the students what to read and then asked questions or gave workbook assignments. The researcher concluded that "whether children's answers were right or wrong was the big concern" (p. 47).

Other studies document that many teachers still spend much of their time asking questions that require nothing more than the recollection of simple facts. One investigator (Sirotnik, 1983) notes that less than 1 percent of the class time spent on questions is devoted to questions that call for a thoughtful reply. Another researcher (Gall, 1984) concludes that only about 20 percent of teachers' questions require students to think. Other research shows that teachers discourage thoughtful comments by giving students only one second to begin answering their questions (Rowe, 1974).

Essentially the same pattern is to be found in all subjects and in all grades. And it is not just the teachers. Studies show that textbooks and workbooks give far greater emphasis to rote learning than to higher-level thinking (e.g., Bettelheim and Zelan, 1982). And a study of standardized science tests (Morgenstern and Renner, 1984) revealed that about 90 percent of the items call for nothing more than simple recall of facts.

Fortunately, a new generation of teachers is rebelling against this outmoded approach to education. They know that industrial-age education is not the solution to the problem that confronts us, but part of the problem. It has not, and cannot, prepare today's youngsters for the complex world that awaits them. We must find ways of teaching students how to analyze facts, generate and organize ideas, defend opinions, make comparisons, draw inferences, evaluate arguments, solve problems. We must, that is, find ways of teaching them how to think.

The search is on. The purpose of this book is to help those interested in joining the search by providing them with a brief look at several ways of teaching thinking. Each of the next eight chapters is devoted to a different approach to teaching thinking in our schools. These eight approaches do not, of course, exhaust the possibilities, but they are representative of the kinds of options available. In writing about them, I have attempted to help the reader explore certain key questions.

What assumptions underlie the program?   Every thinking-skills program rests upon certain distinctive assumptions about thinking and how it should be taught. Often these assumptions are not made explicit and must be inferred from the program materials. One program assumes that poor thinking often results from errors in how situations (problems, for example) are perceived and that, therefore, a thinking program should teach strategies for avoiding perceptual errors. Another program assumes that thinking deficiencies are due to a lack of special learning experiences with parents and other adults and that a thinking program should provide these experiences. Another program rests on the assumption that the rules of good thinking are embedded in language and should be taught through carefully orchestrated dialogue. And one program assumes that thinking is inseparable from the subject about which one thinks, and therefore concludes that thinking instruction should be embedded in every part of the school curriculum.

What are the goals of the program?   Some programs specify very clearly what students are to learn; others are more vague. Some programs attempt to teach many skills; others focus on a few. Some teach general skills (such as being systematic and checking one's work) that apply in many, many situations; others teach specific strategies (such as mnemonics) that are very powerful but can be used in fewer situations. In some programs, the emphasis is on the emotional aspects of thinking, such as the way prejudices can affect judgment, while in other programs the focus is more intellectual.

How is thinking to be taught?   What sort of methods and materials are to be used? What is the role of the teacher? The programs differ dramatically in how they attempt to teach thinking. Some approach the problem by having the students work with familiar classroom materials, while in other programs the students work at tasks bearing little or no resemblance to classroom activities. Some programs are meant to be offered in a special thinking course or (as is more often the case) as a unit in some part of the standard curriculum, such as English or social studies, while another attempts to integrate thinking instruction into regular classwork. The role of practice also varies from program to program. In some cases great emphasis is placed upon practice, but in others more attention is given to ensuring understanding. Some programs have students work alone on exercises, while others have them work in pairs or small groups. In certain cases the teacher plays a fairly familiar role as lecturer and discussion leader, but in other cases the teacher's job is to get the students started and then slip into the background, emerging only when special problems arise.

Who is to be taught?   What is the audience for the program? Are all students to be taught, or merely those with particular characteristics? Some programs are thought to be appropriate for students across several grade levels; others are aimed at students in one or two grades. Some programs are intended for students who are behind their age mates in thinking ability; others are used with students of virtually all ability levels. Some programs offer hints on ways to adapt the program to special students, such as the gifted, slow learners, or those with reading disabilities, while others concentrate upon the "typical" student and leave it to the teacher to adapt the program to special audiences.

Who is to teach thinking?   Do teachers need special training? What personal qualities must they have? Again, the programs offer very different answers to these questions. Some programs insist that to be effective the teacher must undergo extensive training, while others believe that no special training is necessary. Similarly, some programs identify personal characteristics that are judged to be essential to the success of the program; others imply that almost any teacher who is willing to use the program will be successful.

What benefits is the program said to produce?   Does the program claim to raise IQs? Achievement test scores? Special measures of thinking? Are students said to perform better in their regular classes? What evidence is there to support these claims? It is extremely difficult to do good evaluative studies of applied programs in the field. There is the Hawthorne effect to consider, the influence of teacher expectations, and countless uncontrolled variables such as student illness and transferal, teacher reassignment, and so on. I make no attempt to review all the evidence regarding the effects of the programs described here; rather, my goal is to provide a representative sample of the evidence available so that the reader may make a preliminary judgment about a program's probable effects.

What special problems will there be?   Will parents and other members of the community find certain aspects of the program objectionable? Will teacher training present special problems? Will implementation of the program require that some part of the present curriculum be dropped? No doubt the answers to such questions depend as much upon the users of a program as upon the program itself. Resistance from the community, for example, depends in part upon how the program is presented, whether there are public meetings at which questions can be answered, and whether the program is voluntary or compulsory. Teacher support may vary greatly with the extent to which teachers are allowed to participate in program selection. Still, each program may be expected to bring with it certain problems. Some programs, for example, engage the student in the discussion of sensitive topics (such as school prayer and racial prejudice) and may be more likely to arouse antipathy than others. Some have limited "face validity"; that is, they do not *look* as though they would work. Such programs may be rejected before they have been fairly tried. Still others require subtleties in their administration that are not easily learned.

In the chapters that follow I have provided information concerning each of these seven questions for eight approaches to teaching thinking.[5] This information has been gleaned from careful study of program materials, manuals, and research reports and from conversations with the program developers and other experts. I have tried to avoid passing judgment upon the programs, since it is not my intention to steer the reader away from certain ones, nor to "sell" others. Instead, I have tried to provide the information the reader will need to make his or her own judgments about which of these programs deserve further attention. It is my hope that after reading the pages that follow, the reader will be better equipped to become an active member of the thinking movement.

2 CoRT Thinking Lessons

The scene is a classroom in Sydney, Australia. The students are ten-year-olds, and the teacher has just asked them whether they would like to be paid five dollars a week for attending school. All thirty children raise their hands, and eagerly give their reasons. "We would use the money to buy candy." "Having money is more grown-up." "We wouldn't have to ask our parents for money every time we wanted something."

Now the teacher tells the students about a way of thinking about problems of this sort called PMI, short for Plus, Minus, and Interesting. Working in small groups, the students list all of the good points about the idea, then the disadvantages, and finally the features that are not easily classified as either plus or minus, but are worthy of notice. After only four minutes of work the teacher asks for reactions. The good points are as before, but now the students mention all sorts of drawbacks to being paid. "Our parents would stop giving us allowance." "The bigger boys might beat up the smaller ones and take their money." "Adults might not give us presents, since we could buy our own things." After listing the pluses, minuses, and interesting points on the board, the teacher asks again how many favor the idea of being paid. This time only one student raises his hand. Twenty-nine students have changed their minds.[1]

The students in this class have just had their first CoRT Thinking lesson. Their teacher has been Edward deBono, creator of the program and director of the Cognitive Research Trust, from which CoRT takes its name. DeBono is a British citizen, born on Malta when that Mediterranean island was a colony of the United Kingdom. After earning an M.D. and then a Ph.D. (in systems behavior), he worked as a kind of creative-thinking consultant for architects,

CoRT THINKING LESSONS

Principal developer: Edward deBono, M.D., Ph.D., Director, Cognitive Research Trust, Cambridge, U.K.

Assumptions: There are two stages in thinking: perception and analysis. Poor thinking often is due to errors in perception, rather than analysis. Perceptual skills are neglected by schools and therefore deserve greater attention in thinking programs.

Goals: Although analytical thinking is covered, the emphasis is on improving perceptual thinking through the use of "tools," such as PMI (Plus, Minus, Interesting) and C&S (Consequences and Sequels), which draw attention to the perceptual stage of thinking.

Methods and materials: Practice through group and class discussion in use of perceptual tools on real-life problems. One fast-paced lesson per week for two years.

Audience: Most commonly used with children between nine and twelve; all ability levels.

Teacher qualifications: Formal training is optional; for information on workshops, contact Edward deBono Resource Center, 4 Canal Road, Pelham Manor, NY 10803.

Benefits claimed: Students become more flexible, are likely to see more sides to an issue, more alternatives to a problem.

Special problems: Older students find tools obvious; some object to tool acronyms; repetitive activities may become boring.

Publisher: Pergamon Press, Inc., Fairview Park, Elmsford, NY 10523.

designers, scientists, engineers, lawyers, administrators, armed forces personnel, and business executives in various corporations. In the course of this work he found that most people took thinking to be practically synonymous with reasoning. Yet he found that people who were quite capable of logical thinking dealt with many of their daily tasks in an inefficient, albeit "reasonable" way. They would, for instance, use logic to defend decisions or problem solutions they had reached without really examining the situation. They were like the ten-year-olds who so readily agreed that being paid for school attendance was a good idea because they never really considered the possibility that it might *not* be a good idea.

Assumptions and Goals

DeBono came to the conclusion that there were two kinds of thinking, each representing relatively distinct stages in the thinking process: analytical thinking and perceptual thinking.[2] Analytical (or logical) thinking, says deBono, is necessarily preceded by perceptual thinking. DeBono (1985) draws the analogy of crossing a room to answer a phone. If it is dark, one must apply logic: there is a chair to the left, a table to the right, a lamp in the corner, remember the footstool. . . . But in the daylight, none of this is necessary: We see clearly what to do. The point is that logic builds upon the perception of a situation. The better students perceive, the more appropriate their analysis will be. In other words, while one may use logic to find one's way across a dark room, a better solution is to turn on the lights.

Analytical thinking, deBono admits, is an important skill, but he believes that perceptual thinking is often the source of many errors in thinking. He (1976) offers this hypothetical example: A doctor sees a patient complaining of stomach pain. The doctor prescribes antacids, gives some advice concerning diet, and asks the patient to come back in two weeks. A few hours later the patient has a heart attack. There was nothing wrong with the doctor's logic: It is appropriate to think that stomach pain is a symptom of digestive disorder (an ulcer, perhaps), and this leads logically to the treatment plan. The flaw, deBono asserts, is in the perceptual stage, the stage at which the patient's complaint was taken to be a stomach pain. DeBono argues that, had the doctor explored the situation a bit more by asking, for example, when the pains occurred (before eating? during exercising?), he might have taken a more effective course of action.

According to deBono, the errors that occur during perception are by-products of the nature of the brain as a pattern-making and pattern-using system. The physical events that act upon the nervous system may be independent, discrete stimuli, but they are never allowed to remain so once they reach the brain. People do not see merely light waves of a particular length, they see a shiny red apple; sound waves are heard as a friend's voice, and so on. "The mind is full of patterns created by experience and knowledge," deBono (1976, p. 94) writes, and these patterns impose structure upon the environment. The system works well, says deBono, but it has its problems. Chief among them is that the patterns are restrictive. A new, much more efficient pattern might be missed because of the overpowering influence of an established pattern. Some information may be completely neglected because it does not fit into an existing pattern.[3]

The way around such problems, deBono reasons, is to perform an activity that focuses attention on the perceptual stage of thought. DeBono (1976) offers the example of a parent teaching children to cross the street safely. He notes that there is little point in telling children not to cross the street if they see a car coming; they probably already know that much. The problem is to get them to see the car. Parents do this by teaching children to look to the left and then to the right before crossing streets. This procedure (look left, then right) is what deBono calls an "attention-directing tool." PMI is another attention-directing tool. It is a procedure that directs attention to aspects of the situation that might otherwise be neglected.

DeBono notes that perceptual tools such as PMI are very simple. They are easily learned and easily used by almost anyone, regardless of their academic background or their intellectual talents. In fact, they are rather obvious. "Everyone knows," deBono (1976) writes, "that it is a good thing to look at the advantages and disadvantages of an idea. But very few people actually do look at the advantages and disadvantages when it seems obvious at first glance that the idea is a good or bad one. Yet this is precisely the situation in which such an examination is most required" (p. 118). A case in point: the question mentioned earlier of whether students should be paid for attending school. To the students, this seemed such an obviously desirable idea that not one student in thirty thought to look for any drawbacks it might have. Thus, argues deBono, thinking tools do not have to be complex to be worth studying.

The problem is not so much that students must be taught how to use such tools, but to get them to make a habit of using them. One of the things that keeps parents awake at night is that, even though they have taught their children how to look left and right before crossing a street, and even though their children understand this procedure, they may nevertheless cross the street without looking. So it is with all attention-directors: They are of little value if they are not used. A vital question to one who would improve thinking is, then, How do we get students to apply the tools they have learned? The answer, says deBono, is as simple as the tools themselves: practice. If the tools are simple, then it takes almost no time at all to instruct students in their use. The real problem is to make the use of the tools automatic, and this can be done only through practice. Thus, parents who would have children look left and right before crossing a street should not discourage the child from crossing streets. On the contrary, they should see to it that the children get lots of practice, practice supervised by an adult or an older child who will see to it that the youngsters *use* the tool. It is only through such deliberate, supervised practice that the use of the tool will become automatic. "Use can come only from habit," writes deBono (1976), "and habit can come only from practice" (p. 138).

Thinking along these lines, deBono set out to design a thinking program that would meet three criteria: First, it must concentrate on perceptual rather than analytical thinking;[4] second, it must teach students how to use simple tools for directing attention to aspects of a situation that might otherwise be neglected; third, the program must devote most of its time to providing practice so that the use of the tools becomes automatic. What he came up with was *CoRT Thinking* (deBono, 1975).

Methods and Materials

The CoRT Thinking program consists of sixty lessons organized into six units. Each unit deals with a particular kind of situation and attempts to teach students to use certain thinking tools when faced with those situations. The first unit, called CoRT I, attempts to improve the breadth of student perception. The ten lessons are aimed at encouraging pupils to look more widely at a situation. The lessons provide instruction and practice in operations that a student can perform to achieve this goal. The first lesson deals with doing a PMI. Other lessons cover other ways of examining an idea carefully. For instance, lesson four is on the tool called C&S, Consequences and Sequels. This lesson teaches the student to consider what might happen if an idea were implemented or a discovery made. It involves listing the immediate consequences, the short-term consequences (one to five years), the medium-term consequences (five to twenty-five years), and the long-term consequences (over twenty-five years). As an example, the students are told about the introduction of rabbits into Australia as a game animal. The immediate consequences of this act were good (for the hunters, that is), but as the prolific creatures multiplied, the long-term consequences were quite unfavorable. It is easy to think of other situations in which doing a C&S might have been helpful. One wonders, for example, what the status of nuclear power would be today if planners had more carefully considered long-term consequences. Would they have foreseen the problems now faced in finding suitable ways of storing radioactive wastes?

CoRT II is devoted to organization: the need to confront problems in a systematic way. The lessons "equip a pupil to think more effectively about a subject instead of drifting from idea to idea . . ." (p. 1). Each CoRT II lesson involves asking a question in a deliberate manner. For example, students learn to analyze a situation by asking the question, "How can I divide this up?" They learn to make comparisons by asking, "What is this like? In what way are they similar? In what way are they different?" And they learn to assess their progress by asking, "What is the conclusion?" Nothing in the lessons will help students answer these questions (they will not, for instance, teach students how to divide something up); the goal is simply to teach the students to ask the questions.

CoRT III has to do with the thinking involved in interactions between two or more people. Instead of thinking about their own ideas, as in CoRT I and CoRT II, the students are to think about the thinking of other people. For instance, one lesson teaches students to do an ADI when there is a disagreement. Doing an ADI means identifying and listing the points on which the two sides Agree, the points on which they Disagree, and the points that are Irrelevant to the argument. One practice item for this procedure concerns a debate over the effects of televised violence on young people. Various points are made by the two sides, and the students try to decide which of these points indicate agreement, which indicate disagreement, and which are irrelevant.

CoRT IV is the creativity unit. One lesson teaches the student to perform a procedure called Random Input. To generate new ideas, the student learns, it is helpful to bring in something that is unconnected with the subject. By way of example, deBono suggests that a person trying to come up with new ideas about cigarettes might use as the random input the word *soap*. Soap suggests freshness, and freshness suggests spring, and spring suggests flowers. Perhaps, deBono suggests, cigarettes should contain flower seeds so that when they are thrown away, flowers will spring up. He adds that students can come up with random words by looking at the objects around them or by randomly putting a finger on a newspaper and using the nearest noun. Random input gives students a concrete way of generating new ideas. Another lesson in CoRT IV teaches a tool called Dominant Idea. This tool involves looking at something and asking "What is the dominant idea here?" and "Can I escape from it?" Consider, deBono suggests, the railroads. The dominant idea in running a railroad is that of moving people or objects from one place to another. If one escapes from this dominant idea, it is possible to consider other possibilities: that railroads might provide entertainment, for example. The student practices this procedure by identifying the dominant idea behind a topic and then trying to escape from it.

CoRT V concentrates on the roles of information and feeling in thinking. The purpose of the lessons is to make the pupils aware of the information and feeling content of situations. One lesson that deals with information teaches the student to do a FI-FO. The student first writes down all of the information that is in the situation (FI); next the student writes down all the information that has been left out (FO). In a lesson called Emotions, the student is told that emotions are more important than anything else in thinking. The student learns also that there are two kinds of emotions: ordinary emotions, or EM (such as anger, love, and fear), and ego-emotions, or EG (pride, power, and insecurity). Practice items include a situation in which a bus breaks down causing a girl to be late getting home from school. The student is asked how the girl's father will react to this (a) if he is pleased with his daughter because she has done well in her exams, and (b) if he is displeased with her because she stayed out too late the night before. The point is to draw the student's attention to how the father's emotions will affect the way he reacts to the situation.

The final unit, CoRT VI, differs from the preceding units. Instead of providing instruction and practice in thinking tools, it provides a step-by-step plan for thinking through a problem. The first three steps have to do with identifying the topic under study; they are the sort of things teachers would like every student to do before writing an essay test or a term paper, since they should help the student clearly define the topic to be worked on. The next five steps are

> PURPOSE: determining the reason for thinking about a topic
> INPUT: gathering information about the problem
> SOLUTION: identifying possible solutions
> CHOICE: picking the best of the available solutions
> OPERATION: deciding how the solution can be put into operation

In going through this plan, the student may use the tools learned in the previous units. For example, in choosing a solution, the student is asked to consider the consequences of each solution and to list the advantages and disadvantages of each. (However, no mention is made of the terms C&S or PMI.)

Students ordinarily complete one CoRT lesson each week. A typical lesson lasts between thirty and fifty minutes and moves through five stages. The *Introduction* to a lesson begins when the teacher distributes the "notes" for that day's lesson. The notes come in the form of a four-page leaflet (see figure 1) that describes the tool to be learned, gives examples of it, and provides practice items and other material. For example, the very first lesson of the program is on PMI. The leaflet explains the procedure this way: "Instead of just saying that you like an idea, or don't like it, you can use a PMI. When you use a PMI, you give the good points first, then the bad points, and then the points which are neither good nor bad, but are interesting. You can use a PMI as a way of treating ideas, suggestions, and proposals. You can ask someone else to do a PMI on an idea or you may be asked to do one yourself."

This description is followed by an example illustrating the use of the procedure. In the PMI lesson, the example is the idea that seats should be removed from buses. There follows a list of the pluses (e.g., more people could get on each bus), minuses (passengers would fall when the bus stopped suddenly), and interesting points (there might be two types of buses, one with seats and one without). Once the students have read the introduction, the teacher discusses the tool briefly and provides one or two additional examples. Altogether the introductory stage is to take no more than five minutes.

In the *Practice* stage the students, working in small groups, use the tool under study on a practice item. One practice item in the PMI leaflet is the idea that every student should spend three months every year earning money. One member of each group may be appointed to record the ideas generated by the group while doing a PMI on this proposal. The teacher allows only one to five minutes for group discussion, and then asks for ideas, usually calling on one person from a given group. Other students in that group or in other groups may make comments, but these are for the most part to be observations missed by the first speaker. There is *not* to be a general discussion, and arguments or debates should be avoided.[5] As points are made by the students, the teacher may write them on the board. The teacher also may comment on the quality of specific ideas. The teacher presses the students to work quickly and makes no attempt to give everyone a chance to speak. Before the students have exhausted the possibilities of the first practice item, the teacher turns their attention to the second.

Although five practice items are listed in the leaflet, the students ordinarily work on only two or three. The choice of the items is

Figure 1. The cover and first page of the CoRT Thinking Notes for AGO, from CoRT I.

AGO: OBJECTIVES

AGO = Aims, Goals, Objectives

You can do something out of habit, because everyone else is doing it or as a reaction to a situation. These are all 'because' reasons. But there are also times when you do something 'in order to' achieve some purpose or objective. It can help your thinking if you know exactly what you are trying to achieve. It can also help you to understand other people's thinking if you can see their objectives. In certain situations the words 'aims' and 'goals' are more appropriate than objectives but the meaning is the same.

EXAMPLE

A football club has the overall objective of winning the championship. But it could also have the objective of being promoted to the next division or avoiding being relegated to the division below. During a match the objective is to win and this involves the objectives of scoring goals and also preventing goals being scored against you. But there are other objectives as well: for instance to train and build up a powerful team for the future and also to entertain the public who pay to watch the games.

PRACTICE

1. A father is very angry with his daughter so he doubles her pocket money. Why do you think he did this?

2. What would your objectives be if you won £1,000 on the football pools?

3. Everyone has to eat to live. But people have different objectives with regard to food. Do an AGO for the following people: housewife, cook, shopkeeper, food manufacturer, farmer, government.

left to the teacher, who attempts to pick those items best suited to the abilities and interests of the students. The entire practice period lasts about fifteen minutes. The teacher tries to maintain a brisk pace throughout in order to keep attention fixed on the tool itself, rather than on the issues to which the tool is being applied.[6]

After the practice items comes the *Process* stage, a period in which the entire class discusses the tool (the process) being studied. The notes raise certain questions for discussion. For instance, the PMI leaflet asks when a PMI is most useful; whether the students always look at the good and bad points of an idea; whether doing a PMI wastes time; if doing a PMI is easy. The teacher may ask additional questions about the nature of the tool, the need for it, the difficulties in using it, and so on. As always, the pace is supposed to be "crisp and brisk," with the teacher watching carefully to see that the discussion does not get bogged down in philosophical meanderings. The process stage lasts no more than ten minutes.

In the *Principles* stage of the lesson, the students once again work in groups. This time they consider five principles listed in the leaflet concerning the tool under study. For instance, the principles listed in the PMI leaflet include the idea that the PMI tool is important because without it one might reject a good idea that seems bad at first. The teacher asks the students to perform some task concerning the principles. The teacher may, for example, ask the students to pick the most important principle or ask them to add a new principle. There is nothing very profound about any of the principles, and the student is not expected to commit them to memory. The purpose of this stage of the lesson is to get the students to think about the nature of the tool. Once again, the pace is fast; this stage is to be completed in from three to five minutes.

The final stage of a lesson is the *Project*. The leaflet lists additional practice items. Where time permits, the students choose one of these to work on in the manner described earlier. A maximum of fifteen minutes is devoted to this stage. When time is short, the project stage may be ignored or assigned as homework. Or it may be made the subject of an English essay or a class discussion at a later time.

There are variations on the format just described. In particular, deBono mentions role playing, dramatization, drawing, and essay writing. But the focus of the lessons is never these activities but the tool under study. The teacher keeps this focus by maintaining a brisk pace, by cutting off debate and discussions, by repeatedly reminding the student of the tool being studied, and by discouraging the tendency to apply tools used in previous lessons. This last point is based on the belief that new tools will be learned best if they are tested in isolation; hence, while students are encouraged to use the tools outside of the lesson, each lesson is devoted exclusively to one tool. Thus, deBono discourages teachers from reviewing tools covered earlier; his advice is that teachers stick to the tool in the day's lesson.[7] DeBono (1973) compares his lessons in thinking to lessons in tennis. In learning to play tennis one spends a great deal of time practicing various strokes. But one does not merely practice hitting the ball; one practices the forehand, the backhand, the serve, or some other particular stroke. So it should be with learning to think. The student should practice one particular thinking tool, deBono says, and not merely thinking in general.

Another function of the teacher is to provide feedback to the students. DeBono believes that grades probably are not appropriate, but he provides test items so that students and teachers can assess their progress. Teachers also should praise good ideas by saying, for example, "That's a very good point" or "That is a very original idea." They may praise an entire group in the same way. The teacher may also criticize ideas, especially if they suggest that a student is not taking the lesson seriously. While there may be no one right answer, "there are," deBono insists, "many wrong answers, silly answers or trivial answers and the teacher is perfectly justified in treating them as such" (deBono, 1975, p. 14 of *CoRT I Teacher's Manual*). The teacher also may stimulate thinking by asking a student to expand on an idea, clarify an ambiguous statement, or condense a number of points into one idea.

Target Audience

Of course, the nature of the teacher's comments, and in fact the conduct of the entire lesson, have to be appropriate to the students involved. The program most often is used with children between the ages of nine and twelve. However, deBono reports that the program has been used with students as young as five and with adults, including executives in large corporations. The IQs of students who have taken the course have ranged from about 80 to 140. DeBono (1975) admits that it is possible to work with so varied an audience only if teachers adapt the program appropriately.

DeBono offers some guidance on making such adaptations. He suggests, for instance, that younger students be given more guidance, more encouragement, more praise. With these students the teacher may want to read the leaflet material aloud to them, since their reading skills may not be up to the task. And the teacher may want to cover less material in a lesson: perhaps one or two practice exercises and less discussion of the tool, per se. When working with older students, the teacher should be more demanding, more critical of the ideas produced. These students may be dissatisfied with the lack of ordinary content, so the teacher may need to do more to develop the purpose of the lesson so that it does not seem frivolous. Though deBono does not recommend grading student work, he does suggest that older students may respond well to tests, and he provides test items in the handbooks. The tests allow the students to demonstrate their individual achievement. Older students also are more concerned about getting credit for their ideas, so the teacher may want to give them more opportunities to speak before the class as a whole or to work independently.

In general, these same suggestions are said to be appropriate ways of adapting the program to students of more or less ability, with the less talented students working in smaller groups, receiving more guidance and support, and so on. These and other suggestions on how to implement the CoRT program are to be found in deBono's books, especially *Teaching Thinking*, and in the teacher's manual that accompanies each unit.

Teacher Training and Qualifications

More formal training for teachers is harder to come by, but a few of deBono's associates give workshops. DeBono admits that the lack of a training program has certain disadvantages, but he maintains that many teachers have succeeded without special training. The reasons for this, deBono explains, are that the materials themselves are highly structured, and the teacher's manuals are very detailed. Indeed, the manuals do provide much of the kind of material that might be offered through training workshops. There is a discussion of the theoretical underpinnings for CoRT; step-by-step instructions for teaching each lesson; additional practice items to supplement those in the notes; sample answers to the practice items; and a review of the kinds of problems the teacher may incur and suggestions on how to deal with them.

Moreover, deBono maintains, it is the quality of the teacher, not training in the use of a program, that counts most in teaching thinking. The program merely provides a framework for teaching thinking. What is essential, deBono (1976) says, is a teacher who approaches the program with the attitude, "Let's see how we can *make* this work" (p. 152).

Evaluation

Are teachers able to make it work? There certainly has been no lack of attempts. DeBono (1985) says that the CoRT thinking lessons have been used in over five thousand schools in England, Scotland, Wales, Australia, New Zealand, Canada, Spain, Malta, and Nigeria. It is used in one way or another in about 20 percent of British secondary schools (deBono, 1976). In Venezuela, CoRT was tested in a pilot program and is now part of the course of study of all students in grades four, five, and six. Surely, from all this experience, there should be some indication of how well CoRT works.

DeBono believes that there is, and that the indications are that the program works well.[8] His confidence stems primarily from the changes he and others have seen in the everyday behavior of CoRT-trained students. DeBono (1976) gives the example of a nine-year-old girl who asked that her hair be cut short but was then very unhappy with the result. She locked herself in her room to sulk, but the next morning was in good spirits again. She explained that in school she had learned to do a PMI, and she had applied this tool to her situation. Because of it, she realized that her short hair would have many advantages she had not at first seen. DeBono (1975) also says that the effects of training show up in class discussions: Those who have had CoRT thinking stick closer to the topic, are less likely to whisper among themselves, and are more tolerant of views different from their own.

In assessing the value of a program such as CoRT, deBono maintains that such informal evidence is more important than hard data. He adds, however, that more formal studies also provide evidence of the program's value. Such studies compare CoRT-trained students with comparable controls on the examination of an idea. For instance, in one experiment (deBono, 1976), girls aged twelve and thirteen wrote essays on the idea of requiring a year of social-service work from students after they leave school. One group of students had had fourteen CoRT lessons, the other none. The trained students averaged thirty-six ideas, while those in the comparison group averaged fewer than seventeen. DeBono describes a number of similar studies yielding comparable results (see, for example, deBono, 1976, 1985).

Not everyone finds this sort of evidence convincing, however. Among the more skeptical are Peter Polson of the University of Colorado and Robin Jeffries of Carnegie-Mellon University (Polson and Jeffries, 1985). They object to the "informal nature" of such research and to deBono's tendency to describe the studies in sketchy form.[9] They also note that there are no studies on the effects of the entire program; in most studies students have received no more than ten lessons.

There are other problems to be considered. DeBono acknowledges that some teachers and students object to the acronyms (PMI, CAF, OPV) by which the tools are known. They complain that these are a nuisance to learn and add nothing to the usefulness of the techniques, which are really quite familiar to everyone. DeBono's (1985) reply is that the terminology is useful precisely because the tools are familiar to everyone: They help to make familiar processes strange, so that they get the attention they deserve.

A related problem is that students may complain that they already know the things the program teaches. DeBono admits that most students know how to use the thinking tools in CoRT, but he insists that students have not learned to use them. Over and over again deBono argues that learning to think is not so much a matter of learning new procedures, but of forming the habit of using those procedures. It is because of this that "obvious things are far more difficult to teach than anything else" (1976, p. 118).

Another problem is monotony. Virtually all of the lessons follow essentially the same plan. DeBono concedes that this is a problem, and recommends that teachers combat it by keeping the students' attention focused tightly on the tool in each lesson.

The last point suggests that another problem with the program may be an unfavorable student reaction. DeBono reports that student reaction is usually quite positive.[10] But he hints that the program takes some getting used to. "There is no reason at all," deBono (1976) writes, "to suppose that, from the start, the teaching of thinking will be easy, or that it will be rapturously received by the pupils. It may be necessary to go 'uphill' for a while and face awkwardness and other difficulties before things settle down on the other side of the hump" (p. 231). What life is like on the other side of the hump is not detailed, but apparently deBono believes that the atmosphere usually is, and *ought to be*, thoroughly businesslike. In *Teaching Thinking*, for example, deBono writes that "the lessons should be tackled in a sober, matter-of-fact manner" (p. 151).

There are a number of lesser difficulties that CoRT teachers are likely to encounter. DeBono discusses these at some length in the teacher's manuals and elsewhere and offers suggestions for coping with them. But while deBono admits that there are difficulties with the program, he defends its use without hesitation. He maintains that other efforts to teach thinking devote too much time to the analytical stage of thinking, the ability, for example, to find errors in textbook passages. He points out that "life is not written out as textbook passages waiting for reactions. Adults have to plan, decide, choose, construct, take initiative, make things happen" (1984, p. 16). DeBono's aim is nothing less than to help students become adults who plan, decide, choose, construct, take initiative, and make things happen.

3 Productive Thinking Program

The Productive Thinking Program is the end product of work that was begun in 1962 by psychologists Martin Covington, Richard Crutchfield, Lillian Davies, and Robert Olton of the University of California at Berkeley. With support from the Carnegie Corporation and the participation of more than ten thousand elementary students, hundreds of teachers, and dozens of schools, Covington and his colleagues developed and refined a course of study that was finally published in 1974. Since then, the program has been used by thousands of students in hundreds of schools throughout the United States and Canada.

Assumptions and Goals

The program was created to correct what its developers perceived to be a serious deficiency in American schools. "The level of productive thinking displayed by most students," Covington and his colleagues (1974) write in the *Teacher's Guide*, "falls far short of their potential for effective thought" (p. 2). By productive thinking they mean "the use of the mind in an effective, intelligent and creative way directed toward the solution of a problem" (p. 2).

> [Such thinking] is required of the leader of an organization seeking innovative ways to further the goals of his group, of the businessman wrestling with complex decisions about his ever-changing market, of the construction worker figuring out how to overcome an unforeseen difficulty on the job. It is required of the medical scientist searching for a cure for a puzzling disease, of the architect creating a new form for a building, of the student striving to understand facts and concepts in his schoolwork. (p. 2)

PRODUCTIVE THINKING PROGRAM

Principal developer: Martin V. Covington, Ph.D., Professor of Psychology, University of California at Berkeley.

Assumptions: Productive thinking involves five kinds of thinking skills. Improvement in these skills may be accomplished through instruction in general strategies ("thinking guides"). Direct instruction and practice on complex problems are essential. Development of good attitudes fundamental to success.

Goals: To teach use of sixteen thinking guides helpful in productive thinking.

Methods and materials: Students read fifteen booklets with comic book format, and practice thinking guides by answering questions confronting story characters. Class discussion of booklet exercises. Usually taught in one semester.

Audience: Primarily fifth- and sixth-grade students; suitable for all but the slowest learners.

Teacher qualifications: Formal training considered unnecessary.

Benefits claimed: More original ideas, persistence at problem solving, curiosity; use of guides in attacking problems.

Special problems: Vagueness of guides. Some organizational problems in material. Perhaps too many guides.

Publisher: Charles E. Merrill Publishing Co., 1300 Alum Creek Dr., Columbus, OH 43216.

Thinking productively requires the use of reasoning and critical analysis but also imagination and creativity. It involves five kinds of thinking skills: (1) discovering and formulating problems, (2) organizing and using information, (3) generating ideas, (4) evaluating and improving ideas, and (5) creating new perspectives. The Productive Thinking Program attempts to improve these skills by providing training and practice in sixteen general strategies or "thinking guides." For instance, one guide tells the student, "Take time to reflect on a problem before you begin work. Decide exactly what the problem is that you are trying to solve." Another guide advises that a way of generating ideas is to pick out the important objects and persons in a problem and think carefully about each one. A third guide recommends that students evaluate ideas by checking each idea about the solution of a problem with the facts to decide how likely it is.

The *Teacher's Guide* expands upon each of these strategies. Often these comments relate the guide to student behavior familiar to anyone with classroom experience. For instance, on the importance of deciding exactly what the problem is before beginning work, we read that "in the classroom students tend to rush into a problem, without taking time to consider exactly what they are trying to find out and what needs to be done. The result is likely to be confusion, cries for assistance, and, often, premature defeat" (p. 83). Picking out important objects and people in a problem is included since "students often fail to solve a problem because they concentrate on one element of the problem situation while ignoring most or all of the others. They need practice in systematically scanning a problem, noting its important elements and then considering the ideas that each element suggests" (p. 89).

Covington and his colleagues assume that the thinking guides must be taught explicitly if they are to be mastered. "Like the development of any other kind of skill," the *Teacher's Guide* explains, "the development of skills in productive thinking is best promoted by direct, systematic training" (p. 2). The students also need lots of practice, but the practice should not be piecemeal, isolating one skill from another. Rather, practice should involve problems that are "meaningful and challenging to the student and of such complexity as to require the marshalling of all the necessary skills in an organized attack on the problem" (p. 2).[1]

Training and practice in the guides are essential to teaching students how to think productively, but "skill in thinking, no matter how well taught, is not enough. Equally important is the promotion . . . of those positive attitudes and motivations which favor the occurrence of productive thinking" (p. 2f). In other words, "it is not enough to *possess* the necessary skills; the student must be disposed to *use* them" (p. 3).

Methods and Materials

The program that grew from these goals and assumptions comes in the form of fifteen numbered booklets (Covington et al., 1974). Each booklet contains one Basic Lesson and one Problem Set. The lessons teach the students how to use the thinking guides, and the problem sets provide additional opportunities to practice the guides.

Each basic lesson tells a story, told in comic book style, that involves a particular problem (see figure 2). The principal characters are Jim and Lila, two likeable and fairly typical children about eleven or twelve years old, and their Uncle John, a high school science teacher. Jim and Lila are spending a year with their uncle in Elmtown, a small rural community that is just what one might expect from its name.

Basic Lesson 1 introduces the students to the program. The students learn that they will take part in a series of adventures in thinking and that from these adventures they will learn "how detectives and scientists and other good thinkers get their ideas [and] . . . how they use these ideas to make discoveries and to solve mysteries and other interesting kinds of problems" (p. 3). The first of Jim and Lila's adventures is short-lived and ends in dismal failure. On a rainy day they decide to enter a map-making contest, but Jim is unable to come up with any ideas at all, while Lila has ideas but lacks the confidence to share them. These reactions of the characters to their first challenge will be familiar to most students and serve to show them that many others share their frustration and fears when faced with problems. Lesson 1 ends with the defeated children turning for consolation to the television.

The second lesson begins where the first left off, with the children watching a televised news bulletin about a robbery in Elmtown. A

Figure 2. A sample page from *Basic Lesson 3* of the Productive Thinking Program. The students reply to the query in their Reply Notebooks before reading the answer on the next page.

private detective called Mr. Search (his true identity is a secret) investigates and eventually discovers who the culprit is. The contrast between Mr. Search's efforts and those of Jim and Lila in the previous lesson is quite clear: Mr. Search succeeds despite many problems because he uses various thinking guides and because he perseveres. Thinking is thus revealed to the student to be an activity that is full of false starts, dead ends, and mistakes. In contrast to the popular view of thinking as a mysterious and effortless straight-line activity, successful thinking is shown to follow a zigzag course. The lesson ends with the resolution of the robbery mystery, and the emergence of a new mystery (to be taken up in the next lesson)— who is Mr. Search?

In just this way, each lesson presents a mystery of the sort that is apt to appeal to upper-elementary-school students. Jim and Lila attempt to solve the mystery with help from Uncle John. But the lessons are not merely stories about Jim and Lila's efforts to solve mysteries; they are loosely programmed workbooks.[2] Throughout the lessons the students are asked to wrestle with the same challenges that confront the story characters so that they are led through the problem-solving process. They may be asked to state a problem in their own words, to generate ideas, to examine facts, and so on. After each response, feedback is provided so that the students can judge their progress up to that point and take up the next step. "By means of such feedback, and through a succession of carefully planted clues, [the student] is eventually brought to discover the solution for himself" (*Teacher's Guide*, p. 3).[3] For example, in *Basic Lesson 2*, Mr. Search says to the police chief, "Maybe there is still *another* way to look at the problem. . . . Up to this point, we have believed that the money was stolen during the boat trip, but . . . perhaps . . . " Here the narrative interjects: "The detective seems to have a new way to approach the problem. Can you think of what he is about to say?" Following this, the students are presented with a question: "If the money wasn't stolen *during* the trip or *after* the trip, then when might it have been stolen?" (p. 33).

The students write their answers to such questions in a Reply Notebook. (These are not supplied, but any ordinary looseleaf or spiral binder will serve.) The questions are numbered and the students write their replies after the corresponding numbers in their notebooks. After writing their answers to the above question, the students turn to the next page of their booklets and find Mr. Search saying, "Perhaps it was stolen *before* Mr. Burk came onto the boat" (*Basic Lesson 2*, p. 34).

Sometimes the students are asked to detect errors Jim and Lila make when they fail to use a guide. For example, in *Basic Lesson 3*, Lila decides on the basis of rather flimsy evidence that the mayor of Elmtown is Mr. Search. The students are then told that Lila has forgotten an important guide for good thinking and are asked to identify her error from a list of three statements:

a. She is not trying hard enough.
b. She is jumping to conclusions by making up her mind too quickly.
c. She is getting too many ideas. (p. 9)

On the next page, the student finds that the correct answer is that Lila is jumping to conclusions.

The students are asked to use the skills as well as to spot errors. One guide calls for working on problems in a planful way. When Uncle John suggests this guide, Lila and Jim apply it to the Mr. Search problem by listing all the things they know about Mr. Search. At this point, the students are asked to list all the facts they know about Mr. Search. Later on the students use another thinking guide when they check ideas about who Mr. Search might be against the facts they have about him.

As these examples suggest, the questions in the early lessons are easily answered. Later questions are somewhat harder, but by that time the student presumably has acquired greater confidence and skill and is able to answer correctly most of the time. Jim and Lila also improve as they work their way through the various adventures. At first bumbling and full of self-doubt, they gradually gain skill and confidence. By lesson ten they have become quite competent and self-assured, and in the last lesson they solve a mystery on their own, without help from their mentor, Uncle John.

The lessons introduce the thinking guides, but they are not merely taught and discarded. Once introduced, a guide is referred to again and again throughout the remaining lessons, and there are frequent reviews both at the end of each lesson and within certain lessons. In fact, all sixteen guides are covered in the first eleven lessons; the remaining lessons reteach them and provide practice in their use.[4]

Additional practice in the thinking guides is provided by the problem set that follows each lesson. The four or five problems in each set do not involve Jim and Lila and are quite different from the basic lessons, though they call for the same kinds of thinking skills. Many of the problem sets involve real problems taken from the social and natural sciences, history, and human relations.

Sometimes the task is to identify mistakes made by experts in solving problems. In "The Great Piltdown Hoax" (*Problem Set 2*), for example, the student is told about how archeologists were duped into believing that bones planted by a trickster were those of a prehistoric ancestor of man. The facts of the episode are given, and the students are asked why certain facts provided clues that the find was not legitimate. For example:

> In many discoveries of ancient men, the bones are found scattered over a large area. But in the case of the Piltdown Man, his bones were found together, within a few feet of each other.
>   . . . Now complete the rest of the following sentence in your notebook, telling why this fact suggests that a trick had been played.
>   Perhaps someone placed the bones close together so that . . .
> (p. 55)

In other problems, the students are asked to struggle with a famous problem. One such problem asks the students to figure out how typhus is transmitted. The students are told that hospital patients did not catch the disease, even though they might be near someone with typhus. One day a doctor noticed that when typhus patients were admitted to the hospital, their flea-infested clothes were removed and they were bathed. The student is asked to deduce from this observation what the doctor realized—that the disease is transmitted by fleas.

"Jedediah Plans an Adventure" is a human-relations problem. Jedediah Smith, a nineteenth-century American explorer, wanted to open a new trail across the Sierra Nevada mountains. He had to take someone with him, and the student is told about the six men in Jedediah's company from whom he might choose. The

schoolwork. For example, in one exercise students are asked to identify the guides that might be used in writing an essay.[5]

Discussion of problem sets follows the same pattern as lesson discussions. For instance, *Problem Set 8* provides practice in the "just suppose" guide: Just suppose that an unlikely idea were possible, then try to think of how it could be. The teacher's guide suggests discussing "impossible" ideas (such as a sailing vessel that goes over one hundred miles an hour) to bring out the point that many things that once seemed impossible are now commonplace (such as the Hovercraft).

Because of the programmed nature of the materials, it is possible to administer the program without such discussions. All that is required is that the student have the necessary reading skills and be given the basic instructions in the use of the materials. (These include taking time to think, rather than rushing through the materials; not skipping any items; and writing comments in the reply notebook before going on with the story.) Beyond this, say Covington and his coworkers, very little is required. It follows from this that an alternative to classroom use is to let students work on the program individually during their spare time, perhaps as a reward for having completed an assignment. It also may be assigned as homework.

However, the results of the program are said to be better with active teacher participation, and the program developers spell out the kinds of things teachers should strive to do. We have just seen the sort of role the teacher should play in leading class discussions. In addition, the teacher should discourage the students from rushing through the program mechanically without really thinking about the problems or the guides. The teacher also can help by showing the students how the thinking guides may be applied to problems outside the program—in science, mathematics, history, and so on.

Another function of the teacher is to assess student progress. While the students are encouraged to assess their own progress (through reviews and self-quizzes in various lessons), the teacher also can make judgments about how the students are doing. This does not mean, however, giving tests and assigning grades. Grades are said to be inappropriate because the program emphasizes problems that have many acceptable solutions, not just one. Instead, the teacher should look for signs that the skills and attitudes of productive thinking are developing. These signs include an increased tendency toward original ideas, a willingness to stick with a problem, greater curiosity, and use of the thinking guides in solving problems. Such signs may be found in the students' reply notebooks, in comments made during class discussions, and in the quality of standard school assignments. If a deficiency is discovered, the teacher can make a point of providing remedial practice or concentrate class discussions on the neglected skill.

Teacher Training and Qualifications

The developers of the Productive Thinking Program have great confidence in the ability of well-motivated teachers to perform their role in the program. In addition to the suggestions described above, the *Teacher's Guide* provides background information and supplementary materials and resources. It recommends that teachers prepare for a class period by reading over the lesson or problem set ahead of time, including the material on objectives and main points covered in the guide. It advises teachers to prepare for class discussions by reading the suggested discussion questions for each lesson and problem set and by scanning the students' reply notebooks for other interesting topics. Except for a willingness to read the *Teacher's Guide* and follow its recommendations, then, no special training or characteristics are required of teachers.

Target Audience

Neither must the students meet special requirements. The program is said to be well within the abilities of most fifth- and sixth-grade students. Moreover, according to Covington and his colleagues, virtually all these students can benefit from training in productive thinking. Slow-learning students, for example, may study Productive Thinking as a remedial program, while gifted students might use it for enrichment purposes. And since the problems and exercises in the program are challenging and even entertaining, it may help to motivate interest in schoolwork among underachievers.

Evaluation

Many of those who have used Productive Thinking are confident that time spent on the program is time well spent. "The reactions of the thousands of students and hundreds of teachers," Covington and his colleagues write, "have been consistently favorable and often quite enthusiastic" (*Teacher's Guide*, p. 9). They give as evidence statements by teachers who have used the program. One reported that "we were able to see considerable differences in the children's attack on science problems." Children who had not had the program "didn't react adequately or excitedly about posed hypotheses, whereas those children" who had used the program "systematically analyzed the problem and in most cases were able to solve it and to retain the learning" (p. 9). Another teacher wrote, "I noticed evidence of critical-thinking skills being used in science and math and in problems that occur in daily school life" (p. 10).

According to the *Teacher's Guide*, many teachers have claimed that if they begin the program early in the year, it produces a kind of "class heritage." That is, the skills and attitudes learned in the program can be called upon across the curriculum throughout the school year. The teacher may ask, for example, "What would Jim and Lila do?" as a way of helping the children deal with a problem in their regular course work. Or the teacher may call upon one of the guides by saying, for example, "Let's not jump to conclusions," or "Is there another way of looking at the problem?"

The students themselves reportedly find the program both enjoyable and helpful. "The numerous comments by the children leave no doubt concerning their enthusiasm for the program," a teacher writes. "Children who generally have to be prodded became completely absorbed. One boy told me that this was the first time he had ever enjoyed schoolwork" (*Teacher's Guide*, p. 10). In one study (Olton and Crutchfield, 1969), two hundred fifth and sixth graders reacted to questions about the program. Ninety-two percent said that their thinking had improved at least slightly, and half of those said that it had improved a lot. Seventy-two percent said that they enjoyed thinking more, and 91 percent said that next year's students should be given the program. Perhaps the most profound changes in the children, however, are said to be in their attitudes about themselves. A fifth grader wrote, "Now I see that I'm not dumb; I just didn't know how to use my mind" (*Teacher's Guide*, p. 10).

Experimental studies on the benefits of the Productive Thinking Program are cited in the *Teacher's Guide* but are not described in any detail. The results of these studies are said to be uniformly positive. When students who had the program were compared to matched controls, the trained students outperformed their untrained peers on measures of productive thinking. They were, for example, better able to recognize puzzling facts, ask relevant questions, generate good ideas, see problems in new ways, evaluate ideas, and solve problems. Students ranging in ability from slightly below average to above average benefited, and the advantage of the trained students over control students held even when the students were retested the following year. In a separate review of the research, Covington (1985) concludes that the program leads to "substantial improvements" in thinking (p. 407).[6]

There are, nevertheless, certain weaknesses in the program. The thinking guides are meant to be quite general (that is, they apply to a wide variety of problems), and they tend to be rather vague. One guide, for example, advises students to think of unusual ideas. But what constitutes an unusual idea? And how does one think of them? What, specifically, is one to *do* to produce unusual ideas? Or take the suggestion that students pick out all the important objects and persons in a problem and think carefully about each one. How does one decide which objects and persons are important? And what exactly does it mean to think carefully about these items? What does one *do* when thinking carefully? Similarly, it is all very well to tell students not to jump to conclusions, but how are students to distinguish between jumping to conclusions and solving problems quickly? And so on. Each of the guides is useful only to the extent that the student is able to translate it into concrete and skillful behavior, but neither the *Teacher's Guide* nor the lessons specify how this translation is to be done.[7]

Covington replies to this criticism by pointing out that each guide is practiced on a wide variety of examples, and this practice helps the student master skills that are difficult to describe.[8] It must be admitted that people learn many skills this way. In learning to ride a bicycle, for example, one gets some vague instruction in how to keep one's balance, but the real learning takes place *on the bike*. In just this way, it may be that the subtle particulars of the general skills taught by this program are learned in the process of trying to apply them to specific problems.

A less important problem with the program concerns its organization. While it instructs students to attack problems in a systematic, planful way, the program itself does not always do this. Some guides are introduced in a lesson but not practiced in the accompanying problem set. In one case, students are expected to practice a guide in a problem set before it has been formally introduced in a lesson. And sometimes three or four new guides are added in a single lesson; some teachers might prefer that each lesson introduce only one or two thinking guides.

Covington and his colleagues defend the present arrangement by arguing that real problems are complex and seldom include instructions about which thinking guides will be most appropriate to their solution. It is necessary, therefore, to avoid the common workbook approach in which a student is given a group of problems to solve, all of which may be solved by one particular strategem. The counterargument is that it might be better to begin learning a skill by practicing it in isolation before tackling different kinds of problems requiring different strategies.

Another criticism of the problem is offered by Jim in *Basic Lesson 3*. "It really takes an expert like Mr. Search," he says, "to remember all those guides" (p. 6). Uncle John tells him that practice in using the guides will help him remember them. A better reply is available in the form of a large chart (included with the program) that lists the guides; when posted in clear view, students may refer to it whenever they like.

If students *do* remember and use the guides, there can be little doubt that the program is worthwhile. The late Richard Crutchfield (1965), one of the psychologists who helped develop the program, wrote long ago that the student must acquire general skills, "skills which will enable him to cope effectively with whatever the state of the world is as he will later encounter it" (quoted in Radford and Burton, 1974, p. 118). This is a lofty goal. The Productive Thinking Program is an attempt to help students achieve it.

4 Philosophy for Children

Philosophy for *children*? Surely philosophy is an old person's art, a thing to be studied toward the end of life, or at least well into adulthood. Elementary- and secondary-school students cannot engage in serious intellectual discussions of the nature of truth, beauty, and wisdom. Children are not capable of, much less interested in, debating the mind-body problem. They cannot respond intelligently to the questions, What is death? What is life? What am I? No, we are all agreed, education must be simple, definite, unambiguous. Philosophy is not for children, and everyone knows it.

Everyone did, that is, until Matthew Lipman came along. Now, says Lipman, there are over four thousand American elementary and secondary schools offering philosophy. Parts of his program have been translated into French, Chinese, Hebrew, Spanish, German, Portuguese, Danish, and Arabic. Lipman estimates that over one hundred thousand students have had some part of the Philosophy for Children program.

Lipman's interest in teaching philosophy to children began in 1968 during the student disturbances at Columbia University, where he was teaching. Lipman explains:

> It was a very hard time for me. There was so much rigidity among both students and the university administration, so little communication, so little recourse to reason. I was beginning to have serious doubts about the value of teaching philosophy. It didn't seem to have any impact on what people *did*. I began to think that the problem I was seeing in the university couldn't be solved there, that thinking was something that had to be taught much earlier so that by the time a student graduated from high school, skillful, independent thinking would have become a habit.[1]

PHILOSOPHY FOR CHILDREN

Principal developer: Matthew Lipman, Ph.D., Director, Institute for the Advancement of Philosophy for Children (IAPC).

Assumptions: Thinking well requires the ability to perform numerous reasoning skills, most of which are best learned through the use of language (i.e., dialogue).

Goals: To teach students to reason well and to enjoy thinking for themselves.

Methods and materials: Students meet three times a week for forty minutes to read, do exercises, and talk. Focus of the class is a novel in which the characters discover and model principles of reasoning in the process of exploring philosophical issues. Teachers use a variety of special techniques to model and elicit reasoning skills.

Audience: Materials available for grades three through twelve.

Teacher qualifications: A two-week IAPC workshop is considered minimal training. Teachers should have a philosophical bent.

Benefits claimed: Improved reasoning. More thoughtful approach to problems, including schoolwork.

Special problems: Some parents may object to the discussion of controversial topics; some students dislike the lack of simple answers.

Publisher: Institute for the Advancement of Philosophy for Children, Montclair State College, Upper Montclair, NJ 07043.

Assumptions and Goals

And why does such thinking *not* become a habit? What is wrong with our educational system that it produces so many unthinking people? Lipman (1982b) answers that "we do not sufficiently encourage [the student] to think for himself, to form independent judgments, to be proud of his personal insights, to be proud of having a point of view he can call his own, to be pleased with his prowess in reasoning" (p. 37f). To correct matters, we should make thinking improvement one of the goals of every course. Over and above this, however, there should be a course of study in thinking itself.

> The students need an oasis in which the methodology of philosophy is studied for its own sake. You need that kind of austere, remote practice. The student needs to think about thinking, to study the individual skills of which thinking is composed, just as the pianist needs to study the finger movements of which piano playing is composed.[2]

What are the "finger movements" of thinking? Lipman lists over thirty skills that students should learn, including the ability to draw inferences, make distinctions, uncover assumptions, evaluate reasons, and see analogies.[3] No less important than these skills are the attitudes that dispose the students to use them. Learning these skills and attitudes will make students "more thoughtful, more reflective, more considerate, and more reasonable individuals" (Lipman, Sharp, and Oscanyan, 1980, p. 15).

But how are these skills to be taught? Lipman (1984) answers without hesitation that the "major responsibility" for the improvement of reasoning should be entrusted to philosophy. Lipman does not mean, however, that children should read the works of Aristotle and Kant. He does not propose that children study philosophy, but that they philosophize. The classroom should become a "community of inquiry" where students can engage in dialogue in a spirit of cooperation. Get students talking about substantive matters, about deep, philosophical questions, under the guidance of a skillful and thoughtful teacher, and their thinking will improve. But how is one to get children to wrestle with philosophical issues? The answer was discovered in a carpool.

"I used to take my children to school in a carpool," Lipman explains, "and one day I discussed my dilemma with one of the other drivers, an attorney. She suggested that I teach thinking through stories. The idea intrigued me, and later that day I sat down and wrote the first chapter of *Harry Stottlemeier's Discovery*."[4]

Methods and Materials

Harry (Lipman, 1977) is the centerpiece of what became the Philosophy for Children program. Actually there is no set of materials entitled "Philosophy for Children." The program title is an umbrella term for several related but stand-alone programs. Each program has its own novel, its own teacher's guide, and its own exercises.

Harry is intended for fifth and sixth graders and is the story of how one Harry Stottlemeier, a middle-school student, and his classmates discover some of the rules of reasoning that are embedded in language. The story begins when Harry's mind wanders off during a science class. Mr. Bradley, the instructor, has been talking about the solar system, and Harry gets to dreaming about the sun and all the planets zipping around it. Suddenly Harry is snapped back to the classroom when Mr. Bradley asks him, "What is it that has a long tail, and revolves about the sun once every 77 years?" (p. 1). The correct answer is Halley's comet, but since Harry hasn't been listening he doesn't know this. He remembers Mr. Bradley saying that all planets revolve about the sun. And since the long-tailed object also revolves around the sun, Harry thinks it might be a planet. He offers this answer and is met with the laughter of the other students, who have just heard Mr. Bradley say that comets travel about the sun but are *not* planets.

Just then Harry is saved by the bell, but while he is walking home he tries to figure out where he went wrong in coming up with his answer. Mr. Bradley had said that all planets revolve about the sun, and Halley's comet revolved about the sun, but it wasn't a planet. All planets revolve about the sun, Harry observes, but not everything that revolves about the sun is a planet. Suddenly Harry has an idea:

> A sentence can't be reversed. If you put the last part of a sentence first, it'll no longer be true. For example, take the sentence, "All oaks are trees." If you turn it around, it becomes "All trees are oaks." But that's false. Now, it's true that "all planets revolve about the sun." But if you turn the sentence around and say that "all things that revolve about the sun are planets," then it's no longer true—it's false! (p. 2)

This is Harry's great discovery. He is pleased with his thesis, "Statements become false when reversed," but soon sees it demolished by a new example: "No eagles are lions." Harry realizes that this true statement remains true when reversed. Momentarily demoralized, Harry and a classmate soon discover a new rule: "That's it! If a true sentence begins with the word *no*, then its reverse is also true. But if it begins with the word *all*, then its reverse is false" (p. 4).

Harry immediately finds practical use for his new discoveries. His mother is talking with a neighbor, Mrs. Olson, who suggests that a Mrs. Bates is radical because radicals talk about how we ought to help the poor, and Mrs. Bates talks about helping the poor. Suddenly Harry realizes that Mrs. Olson has made a mistake, that it may be true that "all radicals want to help the poor," but its reverse, "everyone who wants to help the poor is a radical," is not true.

This ends the first chapter of *Harry*, but the journey and the discoveries continue through each of the following sixteen chapters of the little book. Along the way the discoveries are applied to real-life situations of interest to children. For example, the characters come to realize the importance of defining one's terms in precise ways:

> Mrs. Halsey [a teacher] was seated at her desk, which really looked like a small mountain of papers and books. She nodded at Lisa, then looked out the window again.
>
> "Lisa," she asked, "would you help me? I've got to assign a topic for the themes for this weekend, but I'm not happy with any of the ideas I've had."

"Like what?" Lisa wanted to know.

"Well, how would you like to write a paper on the topic, 'The Greatest Thing in the World'?"

Lisa stuck her lower lip out very far, reflected for a moment, and then said, "Yiiich!"

"Yiiich?" repeated Mrs. Halsey.

"I mean, I wouldn't like to," said Lisa. Anyhow, what do you mean, 'greatest'? Biggest? Or most important?"

Mrs. Halsey looked puzzled. Then she exclaimed, "Oh, you're right! It could mean both things, couldn't it?" (p. 15)

Harry also gives attention to such philosophical topics as the nature of thought and of the mind:

Lisa nodded. "My mind, why it's like a world of its own. It's like my room. In my room I have my Barbie dolls on a shelf, and sometimes I pick up one to play with and sometimes another. And I do the same with my thoughts. I have my favorite thoughts. And I have others I don't want to even think about."

"But thoughts aren't *really* real," Jill remarked. "I mean they're not real like the things in your room. My thought of Sandy [a dog] isn't the real Sandy. The real Sandy is all full of fur. But my thought of Sandy isn't furry at all!"

"Well, but it's a real thought," answered Fran.

"Do you mean," Lisa asked Jill, "that if there's something out there that your thought is like, then your thought is just a copy or imitation, and isn't really real? So if there's a dog out there named Sandy, then my thought of the dog isn't really real, because it's just a copy of the dog? But there are lots of thoughts I have that aren't copies of anything."

"Like what?" Jill demanded.

"Like, say, numbers," Jill answered triumphantly. (p. 10f)

The discoveries the children make have not, of course, been made for the first time. The rules of reasoning they discover have been taught for centuries, and the ideas the characters share about thought, thinking, mind, truth, and other philosophical topics can be found in such classics as Plato's *Republic* and René Descartes's *Discourse on Method*. But such famous figures and their works are never mentioned in *Harry*, nor does the standard terminology of philosophy appear. This is quite deliberate and is done "so that

children can come to grips with ideas and not merely with labels"
(Lipman et al., 1980, p. 84).

They "come to grips" three times a week for forty-minute sessions devoted to the reading of *Harry* and the open discussion of
the philosophical issues the novel raises. If we want children to
become reflective adults, Lipman (1985) argues, we should encourage them to be reflective children. And how do we get children to
be reflective? By getting them to talk: "The common assumption
is that reflection generates dialogue when, in fact, it is dialogue that
generates reflection" (Lipman et al., 1980, p. 22). Thus, an important part of the Philosophy for Children program is having the
kinds of discussions the children find modeled in *Harry*.

But it is one thing to write a short novel in which fictional
children discuss abstract philosophical concepts; it is quite another
matter to get *real* children to discuss these same topics. Can children
talk about such matters intelligently? Will they? Lipman's answer
is, they can, they will, and they do. And he points to the transcripts
of classroom discussions to back up what he says. Here, for example,
is part of a classroom discussion of the distinction between differences of degree and differences of kind. The conversation has been
going on for several minutes when the teacher asks whether light
and dark red are a difference of degree or a difference of kind:

MANY VOICES: Difference of degree!
[TEACHER]:   Absolutely sure?
MANY VOICES: Yep. Umhmmm. Difference of degree.
[TEACHER]:   OK. How about . . . uh . . . freezing temperature
    compared to boiling temperature?
CHILD: Difference of degree!
[TEACHER]:   Damp compared to wet?
CHILD: Difference of degree!
[TEACHER]:   We're unanimous . . . [while drawing on the board].
    This is called an acute angle . . . and this is an obtuse angle.
    What would the difference between these two be?
WALT: Difference of kind.
MANY VOICES: Difference of degree! Degree!
[TEACHER]:   Who said a difference of kind? Walt? . . . Why do
    you say its a difference of kind?
WALT: Because they aren't shaped the same.
[TEACHER]:   They aren't shaped the same way.

KAREN: Yeah, but they're both angles, though . . . (Children
   discuss . . . , 1979, p. 60)

After several more minutes of discussion, the teacher turns to
the problem of differences between different individuals, and then
to differences between an individual at one point in time and the
same individual at another point in time. Pretty heady stuff for
middle-school youngsters, right? But, says Lipman, they eat it up.

It doesn't just happen though. You don't get this sort of
thoughtful dialogue among children merely by having them read
a chapter of a philosophical novel and then asking them to talk
philosophically. The success of the program depends upon the
teacher's skill at certain discussion-leading techniques, among them:[5]

ELICITING VIEWS.   The reading material provides a starting point
   for discussion, but the topics to be discussed must seem worthwhile to the students themselves. A good way to begin, Lipman
   suggests, is by asking the students what they found interesting
   in their reading of *Harry*. Those topics might be listed on the
   board to form the agenda for the discussion period. Next the
   teacher asks the students for their views on the first item. If
   the students are reticent, the teacher may prompt them with
   questions such as, "Why did you find that particular incident
   interesting?" or "Are you familiar with incidents of this sort?"
   The goal is to elicit the students' opinions on topics of interest
   to them.
CLARIFICATION AND RESTATEMENT.   Once the students begin
   expressing their views, the teacher can keep things moving by
   helping the students express themselves. This can be done by
   rephrasing what they have said ("If I understand you . . . "),
   or by asking questions ("Do you mean that . . . ?").
SEEKING CONSISTENCY.   An important aspect of rigorous thinking
   is using terms consistently. The teacher can help by pointing
   out inconsistencies: "Earlier, when you used the word *brave*,
   didn't you use it in a different sense from the way you are using it now?" And the teacher may show why consistency is
   important by making observations such as, "Are your views
   really different, or are you saying the same thing in different
   ways?"

SEARCHING FOR ASSUMPTIONS. An important philosophical exercise is that of uncovering the presuppositions on which questions and statements are based. Lipman points out that if someone asks a question about how the world will end, he is making the assumption that the world will end. Teachers can help students search for assumptions by asking them, "Are you assuming that . . . ?" or "Doesn't what you say depend upon the assumption that . . . ?"

INDICATING FALLACIES. It is easy to get the idea that in philosophy all views have parity, that all opinions are equally valid. Lipman rejects such relativism.[6] There are criteria by which views may be judged to be more or less reasonable. Some views are based on logical fallacies, and the teacher is obliged to point these out. If, for instance, a student says, "I wouldn't believe anything she has to say about history. Everyone knows her grandfather served time in jail" (Lipman et al., 1980, p. 120), the teacher ought to point out the flaws of such *ad hominem* attacks.

REQUESTING REASONS. Lipman notes that children often give their views on a topic without ever giving their reasons for those views. They can be encouraged to give reasons by being asked, for example, "Why do you think that . . . ?" or "What makes you say that . . . ?" When students give weak reasons for their beliefs, the teacher should help the student find better reasons, rather than dwell on criticism of the poor ones.

These and other techniques suggested by Lipman can keep a discussion going and at the same time teach students the difference between rigorous and sloppy thinking. But it is absolutely essential, Lipman says, that the teacher not use the techniques to manipulate the students toward the "correct" conclusions. Over and over again, he stresses that the goal of a discussion should be to explore ideas in an atmosphere of open inquiry.

At first, Lipman observes, the student's lack of familiarity with open inquiry will work against the teacher's efforts to establish genuine dialogue. The students are used to having questions answered by authorities, so they may press the teacher to settle knotty philosophical problems. Or the students may decide among themselves that such issues may be settled by a show of hands. In

such instances, the teacher is obliged to point out the inappro-
priateness of these methods to philosophical problems. In essence,
the teacher must insist that students wrestle with issues themselves.[7]
That is what the teacher does in this exchange with three sixth
graders:

> TEACHER: Why do you go to school?
> FIRST STUDENT: To get an education.
> TEACHER: What is an education?
> SECOND STUDENT: Having all the answers.
> TEACHER: Do educated people have all the answers?
> THIRD STUDENT: Sure, they do.
> TEACHER: Am I educated?
> FIRST STUDENT: Sure.
> TEACHER: Do I have all the answers?
> THIRD STUDENT: I don't know. You're always asking us
>   questions.
> TEACHER: So I'm grown up and educated but I ask questions.
>   And you're kids and you give answers, right?
> SECOND STUDENT: You mean, the more educated we become,
>   the more we ask questions instead of give answers? Is that it?
> TEACHER: What do you think? (Lipman et al., 1980, p. 94f)

As students become accustomed to discussion in an atmosphere
of open inquiry, they begin to take over the teacher's role. They
will, for instance, search for underlying assumptions, point out
logical fallacies, ask for the reasons for an opinion, and so on. And
this, Lipman says, is as it should be.

In addition to the discussion-leading techniques, the teacher
may develop student thinking skills by guiding them through various exercises suggested in *Philosophical Inquiry* (Lipman, Sharp, and
Oscanyan, 1979), the teacher's manual that accompanies *Harry*.
For example, much of the first chapter of *Harry* deals with discovering rules about true statements, but how does one determine if
a statement is true? The teacher's manual suggests exercises intended
to help students discover two criteria for judging the truth of a
statement. The students are helped to discover these criteria for
themselves by, for instance, judging the truth of a number of statements such as, "Every circle is round" and "Firemen are usually

brave," and giving their reasons for their decision. This done, the teacher can initiate a discussion about the kinds of reasons given and encourage the students to come up with a generalization about them, namely that some statements are true by definition, and others are true by reason of evidence.

The teacher's manual offers no neat rules about which exercises are to be done or when. These are matters that require the same thoughtfulness as leading a discussion. Lipman does suggest, however, that the exercises should be introduced as the topics emerge in class discussions. The idea is for the exercises to be a way of helping the students understand something that *they*, rather than their teacher, have decided needs to be better understood.

The exercises are *not* tests and are not to be graded. In fact, Lipman feels strongly that students should receive no grade for their philosophy work. Grading and the competition it tends to engender are anathema to the spirit of open and cooperative inquiry that philosophy requires. Nevertheless, the teacher should make an effort to evaluate the progress of the class, so each chapter of the manual concludes with an exercise for the teacher. Usually the exercise consists of a series of questions the teacher should consider. For instance, at the end of chapter one, the teacher is asked to answer the questions, "Do all my students understand the rule about reversing sentences?" and "Have I encouraged my students to give reasons for what they say?" (p. 23).

The materials and activities described thus far are intended for use in grades five and six, but Lipman and his colleagues have prepared materials for other grades as well. Eventually there are to be materials (a novel and a teacher's manual with exercises keyed to the reading material) for each grade level from kindergarten to the last year of high school. The entire program is not yet finished, but what is presently available may be summarized as follows.

Kio and Gus (Lipman, 1982a) is intended primarily for use in grades three and four. The stress is on language, especially the forms of reasoning implicit in everyday conversation. Topics include make-believe and reality, fear and courage, space and time.

Pixie (Lipman, 1981) also is directed at third and fourth graders. The novel and accompanying exercises stress deriving meaning from written material. *Pixie* attempts to build an awareness of relationships—logical, social, familial, aesthetic, causal, mathematical, and the like—and competence in dealing with such relationships. There are, therefore, exercises in literal and figurative comparisons, ratios, similes, metaphors, and analogies.

Harry Stottlemeier's Discovery, already described, is intended for use in the fifth and sixth grades. The stress is on formal and informal logic. *Harry* is pivotal. The materials in the earlier grades are designed to develop the skills necessary to understand *Harry*, and the materials that come after *Harry* are intended to offer opportunities to apply the skills learned from *Harry* to various topics.

The last three books in the program—*Lisa* (Lipman, 1983), *Suki* (Lipman, 1978), and *Mark* (Lipman, 1979)—stress the application of the thinking skills developed in *Harry* to ethical inquiry, language arts, and social studies, respectively. They are for use between the seventh and twelfth grades. In *Lisa*, for example, seventh and eighth graders find Harry and his friends applying their reasoning skills to everyday moral dilemmas, such as whether it is right to take circumstances into account when judging lying and stealing.

Each of these books (not to mention the entire series) represents a lot of philosophizing. It is well to ask whether a lot is too much for some students. Are there certain students on whom the study of philosophy is wasted?

Target Audience

Lipman admits that if the students' reading abilities are below the norm for their grade, they will have difficulty with the novels, just as they would with any other reading material that is too hard for them. Similarly, students with poor verbal skills may have trouble expressing themselves during the discussions. But Lipman rejects the assumption that slower students are incapable of dealing with the material or that underprivileged students will find the material uninteresting or too abstract. To many adults, intellectual inquiry for its own sake may seem useless, but Lipman (1985) notes:

> To the child, it is a breath of fresh air. It means there is nothing wrong with playing with ideas, speculating about possibilities, exploring mysterious concepts. It is precisely [this] absence of

executive or managerial purposiveness, combined, of course, with a gamelike insistence upon rigorous observance of the rules and methods of inquiry, that makes this kind of thinking seem so delightful to children. (pp. 98f)

For whom is the program suited, then? For any student, Lipman answers, who is able to read the novels involved.[8]

Teacher Training and Qualifications

Although it may be true that virtually any student with the necessary language skills may benefit from Philosophy for Children, it is not true that anyone may teach the program beneficially. "As a subject," Lipman (1984) writes, "philosophy is highly teacher-sensitive; not everyone can be sure of teaching it successfully" (p. 53). To be successful, teachers must be committed to free inquiry, have a sincere respect for the opinions and intelligence of students, be able to inspire trust, and have the ability to think on their feet.[9]

Lipman believes that nearly all teachers must, in addition, receive formal training in the techniques involved in teaching the program. What sort of training? Lipman believes that teachers should be taught in the same way as they are expected to teach, so training consists of the same reading, exercises, and discussions the teachers will require of their students.

The training can be obtained from Lipman's Institute for the Advancement of Philosophy for Children (IAPC). Each summer dozens of teachers attend two-week workshops offered by the Institute. In these sessions two trainers (IAPC staff with doctorates in philosophy or education) work with a maximum of twenty teachers. Teachers read *Harry*, do the accompanying exercises, and engage in class discussions of the novel and related topics. They also work through one additional set of materials, such as *Pixie*, and its accompanying exercises. Questions about how to deal with specific problems that a teacher might encounter may be dealt with from time to time in the workshop, but it is important to note that the class discussions do not dwell on how to teach philosophy to children; rather, they consist of the same sort of philosophical inquiry that the teachers will later try to establish in their own classrooms. In essence, teachers learn how to teach the program by *taking* the program.

The two-week workshops are considered minimal training. Lipman prefers that a teacher undergo a one-year training program in which two IAPC trainers visit the teacher's school weekly. Trainers lead them through the course (as in the two-week workshop), and periodically supervise the teachers' efforts to implement the course in their own classrooms. "The art of teaching philosophy to children," Lipman and his colleagues (1980) write, "is not acquired quickly" (p. 125). Nevertheless, Lipman believes that well-motivated, intelligent teachers who have had IAPC training usually are able to teach the course successfully.

Evaluation

What does successfully mean? Lipman believes that the study of philosophy for its own sake is well worthwhile, just as the study of history or literature is worthwhile in and of itself. However, Lipman also believes that the Philosophy for Children program results in an improvement in thinking ability. Is he right?

In one attempt to answer this question (Reed and Henderson, 1982), two fourth-grade classes studied *Harry* twice a week for forty minutes at a time for most of the school year. Two comparable groups of students acted as controls. All students took a test of reasoning skills in the fall and then again in the spring. Both trained and untrained students showed improvement, but those who had studied *Harry* made much more impressive gains. A similar study (summarized in Lipman et al., 1980), conducted by the Educational Testing Service of Princeton, New Jersey, yielded similar results.

Lipman theorizes that the thinking skills that go into an intelligent philosophical dialogue also are essential for success in other academic areas. Hence, the Philosophy for Children program eventually should bring about an improvement in reading, writing, and mathematical skills. There is some evidence that indeed it does. In a Rutgers University study (Haas, 1976; summarized in Lipman et al., 1980), two hundred fifth and sixth graders studied *Harry* over a six-month period, while two hundred students from other schools acted as controls. A comparison of reading scores on the

Metropolitan Achievement Test revealed that those who had studied *Harry* gained an average of eight months in reading ability, while the comparison students advanced five months in the same time.

The numbers tell only part of the story, and many of those who have used the program are convinced that it has benefits beyond those that show up on standardized tests.[10] What surprises many teachers most is the enthusiasm of the students for philosophical issues. One teacher (Brent, 1979) tells of a class in which students discuss the problem of identity. (Would you be *you* if you lost a leg? Would you be a different person if you had been raised by different parents?) She reports that "a calm discussion period it is not, with hands waving, bodies bouncing, faces reddening. Amazingly they are listening to each other" (p. 39).

Or consider this example, offered by a teacher who overheard her fifth-grade students talking during a break:

[FIRST STUDENT]:   The Chinese Communists aren't rational.
[SECOND STUDENT]:   You're crazy. They're also people. And we know people are rational animals, so they are too. . . .
[FIRST STUDENT]:   But the newspapers say that all the time.
[THIRD STUDENT]:   But you know what newspapers say is often wrong. Just look at the ads.
[FIRST STUDENT]:   But you say *often*, not always. (Yang, 1979, p. 13)

This sort of conversation is not what one expects from fifth graders, yet many Philosophy for Children teachers offer similar examples from their experience. Moreover, Lipman claims that this kind of thinking does not stop when the students leave their philosophy classes. "Children who have been taught to be systematically inquisitive and reflective," Lipman and Sharp (1979) write, "naturally tend to import such behavior into the remainder of their learning activities" (p. 48). It is said that students bring their sense of wonder and free inquiry, as well as their improved thinking skills, to their other classes. They may ask their math teacher, "What is number?" or their history teacher, "What is history?" They want to know what a scientific fact is, and on what basis one work of art can be said to be better than another.

There is evidence that the students take their philosophy home with them, as well. One teacher raised the old conundrum, Is there sound if a tree falls in a forest when no one is there? After this the teacher bumped into the mother of one of her pupils in a grocery store. "All I've heard the past two days," the mother said, "is trees falling in the forest" (Roddy and Watras, 1979, p. 8). Apparently when a tree falls in a Philosophy for Children class, the sound can be heard in a great many homes. In one survey (Reed and Henderson, 1982), 80 percent of the students who had studied philosophy said that they talked about their philosophy classes with their parents or other adults.

Teachers and parents cite improvements in social behavior as well as thinking. "Many a shrinking violet," writes one teacher, "turned into a tiger lily. . . . " (Brent, 1979, p. 39). A parent had this to say: "Each session made our child *feel good* about herself and her abilities and she definitely learned to be more critical in her thinking" (Cinquino, 1980, p. 5).

There is no doubt that many students enjoy the program and find it useful. In the survey just cited, 82 percent said they enjoyed the program a lot, and none said that they did not enjoy it at all. Ninety percent said that they wanted to take another course in philosophy, and 82 percent said that the course had helped make their reading for other courses more meaningful.

The program is not, however, without its problems. For one thing, the studies described earlier, and most others in the literature, examine the benefits of studying *Harry* and the attendant exercises with fifth and sixth graders. The materials for the other levels have been developed only recently, so at this writing there is little evidence of the value of teaching philosophy to, say, third graders using *Kio and Gus*, or to ninth graders using *Suki*. And there is as yet no way of estimating the benefits that might accrue to students who begin with *Kio and Gus* in elementary school and continue in the program through *Mark* in grade twelve. There is, however, evidence that the good effects of teaching philosophy fade in time if they are not strengthened by continued use. Lipman (1985) notes that the reasoning gains made by students in one study remained intact for two years, but in a four year follow-up the difference between these students and a comparison group had disappeared.

Another area of difficulty is the possibility that the program will be rejected out of hand or administered in a lackluster way because of preconceptions about the value of philosophy. Lipman (1982b) admits that "if anything is axiomatic about American education, it is that children and philosophy don't mix" (p. 39). Yet he and others who have taught philosophy to children claim that children are generally far more philosophical than adults. They constantly ask why, they question assumptions, they wonder. Nevertheless, the adult bias against philosophy must be overcome if the program is to be implemented effectively.

A related problem is the possibility of the rejection by adults of the very spirit of philosophical inquiry. "Philosophy," Lipman and Sharp (1979) write, "presupposes a commitment to open inquiry, and such inquiry might or might not be welcome in certain areas" (p. 50). Some parents and teachers are content with the concept of education as an indoctrination process, with the adult clearly in the driver's seat. The questioning, wondering, and doubt that philosophy fosters is hateful to them.[11]

Even if the spirit of open inquiry is not rejected at the outset, it may be rejected when the class discussions bear upon sensitive topics. A fundamental principle of the program is that the discussions should deal with matters the students themselves find interesting and important. What happens when those topics include sexual behavior, evolution, school prayer, abortion, and drug use? Will certain parents demand that their children be withdrawn from the class? Will the local PTA bring suit against the school system? Lipman replies that in a dozen years of experience with the program, he has learned of only a few incidents in which parents or community groups raised objections.

One reason for this, Lipman believes, is the strict insistence that the teacher avoid anything that smacks of indoctrination. If, for instance, a student takes a stand for or against hunting, it is not the teacher's function to convince the student that the position (whatever it is) is incorrect. Rather, the teacher's job is to point out the flaws in the student's arguments and help him to discover better reasons for that position. This avoids indoctrination, but it raises another dilemma. Suppose that a student is sympathetic to the beliefs of the Ku Klux Klan. Does the teacher act responsibly by helping the child to find reasons for Klan beliefs?

There may be no solution to problems of this sort, and perhaps this is just as well. For this is a program that is not intended to give teachers or children tidy little truths they can tuck away in a corner of their brains and forget about. It is a program intended to prod children into thinking. And apparently it does have this unsettling effect. One exasperated student remarked, "I wish you'd tell us what is real" (Brent, 1979, p. 39). Another complained, "Sometimes it goes on and on. I feel like we're getting nowhere," and a third said, "It's confusing—like, where's your imagination? In your head? In the air? In your mind? Where is your mind?" (Burnes, 1982, p. 10). Lipman no doubt delights in seeing students puzzled thus, for it means that they are beginning to think for themselves. And that, Lipman believes, is the first step in learning to think well.

5   Odyssey

In March of 1979, the Republic of Venezuela embarked upon a great educational experiment: the development of programs to improve the thinking skills of an entire generation of youngsters. The project was the brainchild of Dr. Luis Alberto Machado, the nation's first Minister for the Development of Human Intelligence. As part of this effort, the government took steps to develop, implement, and evaluate a program for teaching analytical thinking skills. The team that would do this work consisted of members of the Ministry of Education of Venezuela, Harvard University faculty, and members of the staff of Bolt, Beranek and Newman, Inc., a Cambridge, Massachusetts, think tank. The program they developed eventually took the name Odyssey (Harvard University, Bolt Beranek and Newman, and the Ministry of Education of the Republic of Venezuela, in press).

Assumptions and Goals

Their goal in developing Odyssey was to create a program that would enhance the ability of students to perform a wide variety of intellectual tasks, "tasks that require careful observation, deductive or inductive reasoning, the precise use of language, the inferential use of information in memory, hypothesis generation and testing, problem solving, inventiveness and creativity, decision making, and so on" (Nickerson and Adams, 1983, p. 2). These skills would be taught independently of traditional coursework but would be directly applicable to such coursework: "The course is not intended to teach physics or chemistry or biology or mathematics. It is our hope, however, that what the students learn in this course will later facilitate their learning of physics, chemistry, biology, mathematics or anything else" (Nickerson and Adams, 1983, p. 15).

ODYSSEY

Principal developers: An international team of about fifty American and Venezuelan psychologists, educators, and government officials.

Assumptions: Intellectual performance depends upon abilities, methods, knowledge, and attitudes. These are best improved through dialogue and discovery learning.

Goals: To teach skills ("target abilities") needed for a wide variety of intellectual tasks. Includes creative-thinking skills, but emphasis is on reasoning.

Methods and materials: 99 forty-five minute lessons organized into six books. Students have three or four lessons per week over a period of two years. Lessons include dialogue and written exercises.

Audience: Fourth through sixth graders able to read the materials.

Teacher qualifications: Formal training is considered desirable and is offered by the publisher.

Benefits claimed: Improved performance on tasks requiring target abilities. Some improvement on academic aptitude tests.

Special problems: Unclear. Odyssey has not been field tested with American students.

Publisher: Mastery Education Corporation, Watertown, MA 02172.

Odyssey rests upon the assumption that intellectual performance depends upon abilities, methods, knowledge, and attitudes. The term *abilities* refers to activities that are essential to the performance of intellectually demanding tasks. Examples of abilities are comparing and contrasting items, recognizing patterns, drawing valid inferences from stated premises, stating the main idea of a paragraph, and so on. *Methods* are the ways of approaching tasks. They include strategies and heuristics such as checking one's work, rereading a difficult passage, drawing a sketch or diagram to represent a problem, and working on a simpler version of a difficult problem. *Knowledge*, as used here, refers to facts, concepts, or principles that students need to understand. Instruction in traditional course content is not one of the purposes of the course, but it is taught whenever such information is necessary for instruction in thinking. *Attitude* is used to mean any point of view, perspective, or opinion that enhances performance. Examples include a sense of curiosity, respect for the opinions of others, and enthusiasm for learning.

Methods and Materials

To teach the abilities, methods, knowledge, and attitudes necessary for high-level intellectual performance, the program uses 99 forty-five minute lessons. Three or four lessons are offered each week over a period of two years. The lessons are organized into six books, each devoted to a particular theme.

The first and most important book is *Foundations of Reasoning.*[1] As its name suggests, the theme of this book is reasoning. It is divided into five units: The first is on observation and classification; the second focuses on ordering; the third treats hierarchical classification; the fourth is devoted to analogies; and the last deals with spatial reasoning. Each lesson within these units treats some aspect of the unit topic. For example, the unit on observation and classification includes lessons on similarities and differences, groups and essential characteristics, classes and classification, and other topics related to observation.

Each of the five remaining books elaborates on the fundamentals introduced in the first. The second book, *Understanding Language,* deals with word relations (e.g., antonyms, synonyms, analogies); language structure (paragraph structure, main ideas, topic sentences); and reading comprehension (interpreting beliefs, feelings, and goals; understanding different points of view). These units build upon the concepts introduced in the first book, most notably hierarchical classification and analogies.

The third book, *Verbal Reasoning*, has units on assertion and argument. The first includes lessons on the use of diagrams to represent assertions and on counterexamples and contraditions. The second unit offers lessons on the use of diagrams to judge the validity of arguments, on forms of logical arguments, and on constructing and evaluating arguments.

Book four, *Problem Solving*, includes units on different ways of representing problems (statements, tables, diagrams, and so forth), systematic trial and error, and thinking about implications.

Decision Making is the fifth book and covers topics such as the nature of decisions, using information to reduce uncertainty, and analyzing complex situations.

The last book is called *Inventive Thinking*. Its first unit is on design and deals with ways of analyzing and improving designs. The second unit is on procedures as designs, and contains lessons on analyzing, evaluating, and improving procedures. (A procedure is any sequence of steps involved in performing an act, such as telling time or buying something at a store.)

A teacher's manual accompanies each book. Each lesson of the program is described in the appropriate teacher's manual in a standard format consisting of

> RATIONALE: the reason why the lesson is included in the course. Why does the student need to learn what this lesson is supposed to teach?
>
> OBJECTIVES OF THE LESSON: what the lesson is supposed to achieve.
>
> TARGET ABILITIES: the kinds of skills students should be able to demonstrate upon completing the lesson.
>
> MATERIALS: objects needed by the students or teacher during the lesson (scissors, paste, and the like).
>
> CLASSROOM PROCEDURE: what the teacher is to do in teaching the lesson.

A lesson from the *Foundations of Reasoning* book will serve as an illustration. This lesson, called Sequences and Change, deals with various kinds of changes. The rationale for its inclusion is that change is a prominent part of everyday experience. Things tend to move from one place to another or pass through stages, and the ability to recognize and understand such changes is judged to be a fundamental thinking skill.

The objectives of the lesson are (1) to develop the ability to recognize changes and sequences on the basis of specific features; (2) to distinguish among progressive, alternating, and cyclical changes; (3) to promote abstract reasoning; and (4) to have the students explain their responses in terms of abstract elements (relative size or position, for example).

The target abilities for this lesson include the ability to identify the dimensions that vary in changes and sequences; to distinguish among progressive, alternating, and cyclical changes; to recognize the next item in a sequence on the basis of observed dimensional changes; and to explain the relations among the elements in a sequence.

The bulk of the lesson description deals with classroom procedures. The teacher's manual provides detailed suggestions on conducting the lesson. Most of these come in the form of "scripts" of hypothetical classroom dialogue. The teacher is not expected to duplicate this script in class; it merely provides a model for the kind of dialogue the teacher should generate.[2] The idea is to get the students actively involved. The program developers believe that just as "spectators do not become skilled athletes" (Nickerson and Adams, 1983, p. 13), so spectators do not become skilled thinkers. The script offers hints for getting the students to participate in the thinking process. For instance, it suggests that the teacher begin the lesson on change and sequence with an introduction such as this: "The things we experience change from one place to another, turn, become larger, or become smaller. Of course, almost everything around us changes, and being able to understand how things change can be very important to us. Five years ago, what were you like: How have you changed?" (Harvard University et al., in press, *Foundations of Reasoning*).

The students should respond by pointing to changes in their size, shape, and so on. From this point the teacher introduces the notion that change is detectable because of differences in certain features or dimensions (size, brightness) of an object. This then leads to an exploration of the kinds of regular change. The teacher might say: "When something keeps changing little by little with time and never goes back to the way it started, we call it a *progressive* change" (Harvard University et al., in press, *Foundations of Reasoning*).

The discussion of progressive change leads into a similar analysis of alternating change. The teacher follows this with the first set of exercises in the book. These deal with alternating changes, and the teacher begins by working through a sample exercise (see figure 3) with the class:

O[TEACHER]:   Observe the first figure of row one. What does the first box in row one contain?

• [STUDENT]:   A line with a circle on top of it.

O: Look at the second box. What does it contain?

• :   The same line with a circle beneath it.

O: What change has taken place?

• :   The position of the circle has changed from above the line to below the line.

O: Observe the third figure. How has it changed from the second?

• :   The circle returned to the upper part, and it has become larger.

O: Look at the fourth figure. What has happened now?

• :   The circle is again below the line, and it has become smaller.

O: Along how many dimensions have we observed changes? What are they?

• :   Two. The circle has changed positions with respect to the line, from above to below, from below to above, and from above to below. The circle changed size in the third and fourth figures.

O: Yes. One of these changes occurred in all four of the figures, and one only in two. Which is the change that all of these figures share?

• :   The change in the position of the circle.

O: Yes. And would you call the changes in the position of the circle Alternating or Progressive?

• :   Alternating.

O: Yes. The circle moves from above to below to above, repeatedly, so it is an Alternating sequence. (Harvard University et al., in press, *Foundations of Reasoning*).

Figure 3. Exercise from the *Foundations of Reasoning.*

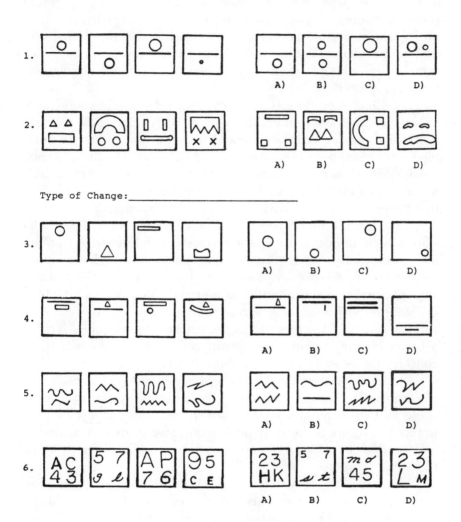

The teacher continues in this way, ending with an examination of the reasons why choice *C* would be the next item in this series (refer to figure 3). After going through a second demonstration problem in this same careful way, the teacher asks the students to do four problems on their own. The teacher then goes over the exercises by asking students to give their answers and the reasons for those answers.

The same procedure is followed for a set of exercises on progressive change, after which the teacher takes up cyclical change. Following these exercises, the teacher asks the students to do three more problems, but in this case the type of change involved is not specified in advance; the student must choose the next item in each sequence and identify the kind of change involved. Complete answers to all exercises are provided in the teacher's manual.

Although the topics covered in other lessons may differ substantially from those of the lesson on change, all lesson descriptions follow essentially the same format: The teacher is told the rationale for the lesson, the objectives to strive for, the target abilities the students are to acquire, and the materials they will need. This information is provided in a page or two, and is followed by a lengthy review of the procedures the teacher should follow. To get a better idea of the substance of the course, it may be helpful to consider the procedures for one more lesson.

In Understanding the Author's Message, a lesson in book two (*Understanding Language*), the idea is that students can better understand written material if they deduce the author's purpose in writing it. The lesson is therefore designed to give students instruction and practice in inferring an author's intentions in different kinds of texts.

The lesson begins with a very brief introduction explaining the subject and its rationale. This includes asking the students about the possible motives for writing a business letter, a personal letter, and a newspaper article.

This introduction is followed with an exercise involving two restaurant ads. There is a fairly detailed examination of the first ad, with the teacher asking questions such as, Why did the author list the kinds of foods served? Why does the ad include the address and phone number of the restaurant? Why does it state that French, English, and German are spoken at the restaurant? And so on. Essentially the same procedure is followed in the examination of the second ad. The exercise ends with the teacher concluding that "we have to think about both the *actual content* of the ad and what the author's *purposes* must have been in order to interpret the messages of the ads" (Harvard University et al., in press, *Understanding Language*).

The teacher now turns to an exercise based on a letter. A student reads the letter aloud, and then the teacher queries the class about the intended message and how the author communicates that message.

Next the teacher turns to the third and fourth exercises. In each of these, the students read a fable and must choose the moral from among four alternatives. The students also are required to justify their choices, and the teacher brings out in the discussion the reasons why the false alternatives fail to represent the author's purpose. After the fourth exercise the teacher helps the students to review what they have learned, and then concludes with a final exercise, another fable.

Remember that the scripts provided in the teacher's manuals are *not* meant to be acted out by the teacher and the students. (The scripts are, of course, available only to the teacher.) They merely provide illustrations of the kinds of points to be covered and the kind of dialogue in which teachers and students should engage. They do make it clear, however, that the Odyssey developers favor the exploration and discovery approach. "The teacher's task," we are told, "is not so much to teach as to facilitate learning" (Nickerson and Adams, 1983, p. 16).

Teachers receive other helpful suggestions. They are advised to avoid providing the answers to questions too soon, to make sure the students have the opportunity to come up with the answers themselves. Teachers should encourage the idea that questions often have more than one answer, and that the reasons for an answer may be just as important as the answer itself. In fact, the teacher's emphasis should be, not upon the answers students give, "but on the ways in which they derive those answers. . . . The thought process behind an answer is what we want to improve, and it is that on which the teacher must focus" (Nickerson and Adams, 1983, p. 35).

It is also recommended that students be encouraged to take the role of teacher, since explaining a concept to someone often helps the explainer get a better grip on the concept.[3] Of course, giving students such opportunities in the classroom means that there is a danger the discussion will stray far from the subject of the lesson. "The astute teacher will attempt to strike a balance between following unanticipated digressions from the planned lessons . . . and guiding the discussion back to the plan (Nickerson and Adams, 1983, p. 28).

The students are not to be graded, either on their class comments or on their worksheets. "In general," comments one of the course developers, "there is very little emphasis on being right or wrong, but much emphasis on trying to figure things out, think things through, etc."[4] While grading, with its punitive implications, is to be avoided, it is considered imperative that efforts to think be rewarded at every opportunity. The net effect is the establishment of a nonthreatening atmosphere that will promote inquisitiveness, a sense of wonder, and curiosity about why things are the way they are.

Teacher Training and Qualifications

No doubt training would be helpful to those teachers who would establish this positive atmosphere. The publisher will provide training to those who plan to adopt the program. However, the teacher's manuals are straightforward, quite explicit, and easy to follow, so it seems likely that well-motivated teachers will be able to master the basic procedures, if not some of the subtleties described above, through careful study of the manuals. No special personal qualities are demanded of teachers, aside from a positive attitude toward the program and thinking instruction.

Target Audience

No special qualities are required of students, either. The program is deemed appropriate for the great majority of students in grades four through six, and perhaps some students in higher level grades. Students may begin the program after the fourth grade, but the authors argue that they must begin with *Foundations of Reasoning*, since it provides the foundation upon which the other books build.

Odyssey is not intended primarily as either a remedial program or an enrichment program; rather, it is intended as one that virtually all students might go through, though slower students might begin later, and faster students sooner.

Evaluation

According to the program developers, those students who go through the program can expect to profit from it in important ways. However, as of this writing, only one study (*Project Intelligence . . . Final Report*, 1983) on the effects of the program has been reported, and that was based on the somewhat different Venezuelan version of the program. The study took place in Barquisimeto, Venezuela, during the 1982–83 school year. Four seventh grade classes in each of six schools participated. Twelve of these classes (four from each of three schools) received training; the other twelve kept to the standard curriculum. There were about 450 students in each of the two groups. Trained students had three or four thinking classes a week. During the course of the year the students completed fifty-six lessons.

All the students took a number of tests at the beginning and end of the school year. To determine whether the course did in fact improve the ability to perform the specific skills covered, the researchers constructed special Target Abilities Tests. To see whether the effects of training carried over to other kinds of tasks, the students took various standardized tests. In analyzing the test results, the researchers computed the differences between the scores at the beginning and end of the school year and compared the average improvement made by the two groups of students. They found that overall the trained students made substantially greater gains than the comparison students. Not surprisingly, the largest differences were on the Target Abilities Tests; trained students improved twice as much as untrained students on these tests. Gains on the standardized tests were more modest for both groups, but the trained students fared better than their peers.

The researchers also solicited comments from teachers, supervisors, and students to get their reactions to the course. One report (Herrnstein, Nickerson, de Sanchez, & Swets, no date) claims that

"the classes gave an observer a sense of forty-five minutes packed
with intellectual activity. . . . [The lessons] created a new, dynamic
interaction between teacher and student, changing the classroom
profoundly for both" (p. 31).

There is, then, at least preliminary evidence that Odyssey can
produce significant improvements in certain kinds of thinking skills.
There are, however, certain limitations that should be kept in mind
by those interested in implementing the program. Any new program
may be expected to have some "bugs" in it, and there is no reason
to think that Odyssey will be an exception. Moreover, the program
has yet to be tested in any formal way with American students and
teachers. The Venezuelan results are encouraging, but differences
in the nature of the programs, the students, and the teachers may
mean that those results will not carry over to American (or other
English-speaking) classrooms.

Odyssey is among the newest of thinking programs to appear.
Its youth brings with it certain disadvantages, but it also brings
the virtue of being a fresh and exciting approach to the problem
of teaching students how to think.

6 Instrumental Enrichment

I have a young man who at the age of fifteen was almost illiterate and who is today a college professor. Another had been almost an imbecile, but today is functioning at a much higher level. I had a guy who had a 55 IQ; after five and a half years of intense training he is now matriculating for university. He's not an A student, but he has Bs and Cs.[1]

This is Reuven Feuerstein (pronounced *foy-er-schtyne*). In slightly twisted English and an eclectic European accent, the Israeli clinical psychologist delights in describing some of his more successful attempts at improving the intellectual performance of those labeled "slow" or "retarded." Out of this work came a program called Instrumental Enrichment (Feuerstein, 1978), a program that is now part of the standard curriculum of some thirty thousand Israeli students.[2]

Feuerstein is the former Director of Psychological Services at Youth Aliyah, an organization for wayward, orphaned, and abandoned children in Israel. Sixtyish, portly, sporting a white beard, a large dark beret, and an impish smile, Feuerstein looks as though he just stepped out of a Tolkien novel. This overgrown Hobbit will sit before you and tell you that intelligence is not carved in cerebral marble but is a soft clay that can be shaped at will, that many youngsters with IQs of 80, 60, or even 40 can, with appropriate training, perform at normal or near-normal levels.

Assumptions and Goals

Feuerstein emigrated from his native Rumania to Israel in 1944 after spending several months in a labor camp. In his new homeland, he worked for Youth Aliyah, which had been set up to cope

INSTRUMENTAL ENRICHMENT

Principal developer: Reuven Feuerstein, Ph.D., former Director of Psychological Services, Youth Aliyah, Jerusalem, Israel.

Assumptions: Students learn to think by means of "mediated learning experiences." A lack of such experiences may result in "cognitive deficiencies." Remediation should consist of providing mediated learning experiences.

Goals: To correct cognitive deficiencies such as impulsivity and lack of appreciation for accuracy; to replace a passive orientation toward the environment with an active one.

Methods and materials: Fifteen units consisting of paper and pencil exercises designed to correct cognitive deficiencies. One-hour classes meet three to five times a week for two to three years. Teacher leads discussion of exercises.

Audience: Ages eleven to adult. Used with various ability levels but best suited to those below grade level.

Teacher qualifications: Teacher training mandatory. Intelligence to meet the challenge of a complex and novel program.

Benefits claimed: Cognitive skills improve; students become less passive; general learning ability increases.

Special problems: Lack of face validity; little progress seen in first year; difficult to administer.

Publisher: University Park Press. Note: Do not contact publisher. Write to R. Feuerstein, 6 Karmon St., Jerusalem, Israel.

with the influx of Jewish children who had survived the Holocaust. Many of these children appeared retarded on standard IQ tests, but Feuerstein wondered whether such tests were fair to students who had spent much of their lives sleeping in doorways and begging for food.[3] He began to teach them and found that many of these "retarded performers," as he came to call them, were far more capable than their IQs suggested. Youngsters who had demonstrated a remarkable ignorance of facts proved that they could acquire them; those who had no grasp of the most basic concepts (such as right and left) readily mastered them; those who showed no evidence of abstract reasoning learned to reason abstractly. Feuerstein came to believe that the initial poor performance of these youngsters was the result of intellectual impoverishment. Specifically, what these and so many retarded performers have in common is a lack of "mediated learning experiences."

In a mediated learning experience a knowledgeable person, usually an adult, intervenes between the person and the environment. The mediator "transforms, reorders, organizes, groups and frames the stimuli in the direction of some specifically intended goal and purpose" (Feuerstein and Jensen, 1980, p. 409). Virtually any experience can become a mediated learning experience if someone intervenes in such a way as to make the experience "transcend itself." The everyday experience of stopping for a traffic light will serve as a simple example. The child who accompanies an adult driver no doubt learns something from the experience itself. But there is much more the child might learn if the adult intervenes. To make this into a mediated learning experience, the adult might point out to the child that the red light means stop and the green light go, and that this arbitrary rule has a rational justification: the need to control traffic. The adult might go on to discuss with the child other situations in which arbitrary rules regulate behavior: driving on the right side of the road, standing in line, raising one's hand in class, and so on. Even simple commands can become mediated learning experiences. By way of example, Feuerstein (1980) points to the difference between saying to a child, "Please buy three bottles of milk," and "Please buy three bottles of milk so that we will have enough left over for tomorrow when the shops are closed" (p. 21). In the first case there is only a command to be obeyed; in the second case the child is made privy to the reasoning behind the command. The specific content of an experience is, according to Feuerstein, unimportant: It makes little difference whether the child is learning the names of the dinosaurs or is asked to close the windows when a storm threatens. What is important is the extent to which the experience offers insight into the thinking required for the task.

According to Feuerstein, then, too few mediated learning experiences result in poor thinking skills, which in turn reduces the individual's ability to profit from everyday learning opportunities. The result is the development of a number of "cognitive deficiencies." These include impulsivity, a lack of verbal skills, failure to use spatial concepts to orient oneself, lack of regard for precision and accuracy, failure to recognize and define problems, failure to make comparisons, failure to appreciate the need for logical evidence, and so on. In one of his books, Feuerstein (1980) describes twenty-one of these cognitive deficiencies. Underlying all of them is a passive approach to the environment: Retarded performers do not recognize that their own intellectual effort may contribute to the successful performance of a task. Feuerstein cites the case of a girl who, when asked how long it took her to get to school, said she did not know. Yet she knew what time she got on the school bus and what time she arrived at school. Moreover, she knew how to do the simple arithmetic necessary to compute the difference. But she did not see that she could produce new information merely by thinking. The retarded performer sees himself at best as a passive receptacle of information, not as someone who generates and uses information.

If this passivity and the more specific cognitive deficiencies are due to a lack of mediated learning experiences, it follows that remediation requires "a massive and systematic supply of mediated learning experiences commensurate with the severity of the condition" (Feuerstein and Jensen, 1980, p. 412).[4] Feuerstein's efforts to construct ways of providing such mediated learning experiences eventually resulted in the development of the Instrumental Enrichment program.[5]

Methods and Materials

Instrumental Enrichment consists of fifteen units or "instruments," so called because each is said to be instrumental in helping youngsters overcome one or more cognitive deficiencies.

ORGANIZATION OF DOTS. In the first instrument, the task is to connect dots so as to construct specified geometric forms (see figure 4). The task is complicated by the fact that the shapes are embedded in an amorphous array of dots and by the fact that the forms overlap.

ORIENTATION IN SPACE, *I, II, III*. In these three instruments, the students are asked to identify the spatial relationships among objects. They may be asked to examine an illustration and note that it depicts a hat *on* a chair or a cat *under* a table. In the process, the students learn the value of terms such as front, back, left, right, up, down, above, below, North, and South.

COMPARISONS. As the name implies, this instrument requires the student to look for similarities and differences between two or more objects or concepts. The dimensions examined are sometimes concrete (size, form, number, color) and sometimes abstract (function, composition, power). A typical item asks the student to indicate how two things (such as a factory and a church, or milk and salt) are alike and how they are different. In another exercise, the student ranks five figures according to how closely they resemble a model.

CATEGORIZATION. These exercises involve identifying the class or category to which an object may be assigned. In one item the student identifies a number of pictured objects, then lists all of those that represent forms of transportation, those that are kinds of clothing, objects that give off light, and so on. In another item, the student is asked to build a zoo. He is shown pictures of various animals, and must devise a plan for organizing the animals sensibly.

ANALYTIC PERCEPTION. Here the task is to break a whole into its component parts. A typical item asks the student to find a simple geometric form (an ovoid, say) that is embedded within a more complex one (a number of overlapping circles and ovoids).

FAMILY RELATIONS. Retarded performers often have little grasp of the abstract meanings of relational terms. Feuerstein (1980) notes that when such youngsters are asked, for example, "How is he your cousin?" they may answer, "Because he helps me" (p. 194). This instrument develops an awareness of the relationships that define such terms. In one item, the student learns the reciprocal relationships between brother and sister and between husband and wife.

Figure 4. The first exercise in the Organization of Dots unit in the Instrumental Enrichment program.

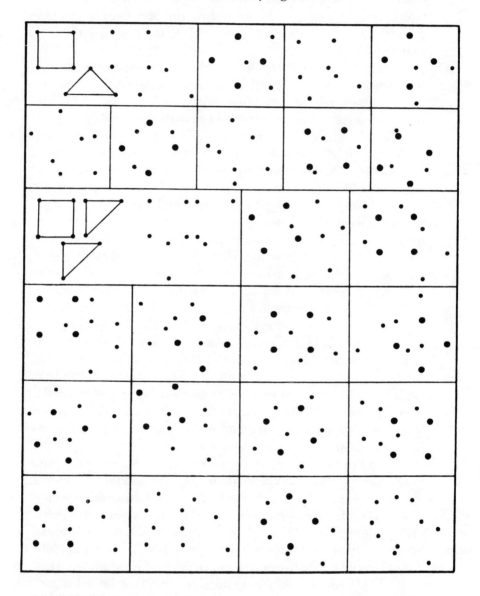

Reprinted with permission of the author and publisher from *Just a Minute . . . Let Me Think.* © 1978 by Reuven Feuerstein.

TEMPORAL RELATIONS.   The sequential nature of time and events is the subject of this instrument. Items include arithmetic problems such as, "A stork flew from Toronto to New York City. On the first day it flew a distance of 15 miles (24 kilometers). On the second day it flew at the same speed, yet covered a distance of 22 miles (35 kilometers). Explain" (Feuerstein, 1978, p. 7).

NUMERICAL PROGRESSIONS.   The exercises in this instrument involve finding relationships among disparate objects and events, including not only arithmetic progressions but figural and common cause-effect relationships. In one item the student is asked to continue a progression of geometric shapes. In another item the problem is to come up with a plausible explanation for the fact that a pot that was once full of water is now empty.

INSTRUCTIONS.   The task here is to read instructions and carry them out. Usually the instructions direct the student to draw various figures. One item states: "On a line draw a triangle, two squares and a circle, not according to size order. The squares are to be equal in size; the triangle is to be larger than the squares and smaller than the circle; and the largest figure is to be on the left side" (Feuerstein, 1978, p. 13).

ILLUSTRATIONS.   The items of this instrument are not to be taken up one after another, as in the other instruments. Instead, they are interspersed among other exercises. The items consist of cartoons, and the student's task is to say what is going on in the scenes depicted and why the cartoons are funny. In one, a janitor's broom handle tears a hole in a painting depicting an ocean scene, and a torrent of water pours from the painting onto the floor.

REPRESENTATIONAL STENCIL DESIGN.   In this instrument the student's task is to figure out how to construct a design that is identical to a model. Colored stencils are printed on a poster and the student must specify which stencils must be used and in what order to reproduce the model.

TRANSITIVE RELATIONS.   These items require making inferences from relations among objects or events that can be expressed as greater than, equal to, or less than. A typical problem reads, in part, "Adam likes math more than history, and history less than geography. Is it possible to know which Adam likes more, math or geography?" (Feuerstein, 1978, p. 6).

SYLLOGISMS.   The last instrument deals with formal propositional logic. One of the easier items is

No midgets are giants.

Tom Thumb is a midget.

Conclusion: _____ is not a _____ (Feuerstein, 1978, p. 13).

Harder items involve more abstract concepts, such as geometric forms.

As you can see, most of the instruments are essentially free of traditional academic content. Students may be taught the words *vertical* and *horizontal* in order to work on one instrument, or they may be taught what an analogy is in order to master the items on another. But such concepts are taught merely as prerequisites to teaching thinking skills. One reason traditional content is avoided is that many of the students for whom Instrumental Enrichment is intended come to school-like tasks convinced that they cannot do them. Another advantage of nonacademic material is that it is said to help focus attention on the process of thinking rather than on its products.

Some of the exercises may seem a bit frivolous, but remember that the task itself is relatively unimportant; its purpose is merely to provide the basis for mediated learning experiences through which the students may overcome their cognitive deficiencies. It is not possible, for example, to perform the *Organization of Dots* items correctly if one is impulsive.

The lessons, which increase in difficulty as the course progresses, are administered in hourly sessions three to five times a week over a period of two or three years. The teacher's guide (Feuerstein and Hoffman, 1980) provides detailed instructions for conducting the lessons. Typically, a lesson consists of an introductory discussion, individual work on a page of exercises, a class discussion, and a summary.

During the introductory discussion the teacher provides groundwork for the paper and pencil exercises by helping the students understand the basic concepts involved. For instance, here is part of one class's introduction to the first lesson on categorization:

TEACHER: What is classification?

STUDENTS: Organizing. Putting into order. Putting things to one side. Separating. Putting things into different groups.

TEACHER: What do we ordinarily categorize?

STUDENT: In school, we divide the kids into classes: according to their age and level; according to different teachers; according to the vocational subjects they take.

TEACHER: Other examples, not from school.

STUDENT: In the post office, they separate stamps into airmail and regular and according to their prices and the sets.

TEACHER: The mailman has to sort his mail into areas, and then into buildings and then into apartments. (Feuerstein, 1980, p. 176f)

The introduction, which usually lasts no more than ten minutes, also includes a discussion of the thinking skills required for the performance of the exercises. After the introduction, the students work independently for at least twenty-five minutes on a page of exercises. As they work, the teacher offers help to students who are having difficulty. The student who completes the exercises first becomes a teacher's aide who offers guidance to slower students.

When most students have completed the exercises, the class as a whole discusses them. The teacher and students explore the thought processes involved in performing the task, analyze the difficulties encountered, and note how those difficulties were overcome. Here is an excerpt from a discussion of a lesson from the unit on instructions:

STUDENT: Now when I get sent out on a job interview, I ask who I got to see, because I know he's the only one who's going to know anything about it. I ask where I can find him and what is the best time to see him. Then I ask for the address, and the exact name of the company, and how to get there.

STUDENT: Don't you care what the job is and how much it pays?

STUDENT: Sometimes that's not the most important thing.

TEACHER: Is there a time when the "how much" is important?

STUDENT: Sure. I need to know exactly how much glass I'm gonna need to fix a broken window, because it's gotta fit exact in the frame.

STUDENT: I think how much when I buy something.
STUDENT: How much is important any time you're baking or
   cooking. (Feuerstein, 1980, p. 229f)

This example illustrates the way in which the discussion can focus
on correcting a specific cognitive deficiency, in this case the failure
to appreciate the importance of precision and accuracy.

The lesson concludes with a brief summary. This includes a
restatement of the points covered in the introduction. It points up
the particular goals of the lesson and the extent to which those
goals have been achieved. Initially, the teacher summarizes the
lesson, but later on the students take on this responsibility.

Feuerstein places special emphasis upon the importance of what
he calls bridging: showing the relevance of the skills being learned
to other areas, including schoolwork and everyday experiences.[6] In
the discussion of classification reported earlier, for example, the
teacher bridged by asking the students for examples outside of
school. Similarly, students working on *Analytic Perception* may be
asked by their teacher for examples outside of school in which it
is important to identify the relevant parts.

Although each instrument is designed to help retarded performers overcome certain cognitive deficiencies, there is considerable duplication. In some sense, each of the units is instrumental
in helping the student to control impulsivity, to see the connect-
edness of objects and events, to recognize problems, and to overcome many other cognitive deficiencies. In addition, Instrumental
Enrichment instructors are encouraged to help students apply new
skills to their regular coursework and to other aspects of their lives.
This repetition is necessary, Feuerstein believes, for the retarded
performer's newfound skills to become habitual.

Target Audience

The retarded performers for whom these lessons are intended
are, for the most part, eleven years of age or older and are functioning substantially below their age level. Many of them have IQs
between 75 and 90, the gray twilight between true retardation and
normal intelligence. But Feuerstein also uses the program with

students with much lower IQs. Asked if there is a limit below which Instrumental Enrichment is useless, Feuerstein hedges: "It all depends. . . . We have a good number of children with IQs of 40."[7] The point, Feuerstein seems to think, is not how great the deficit is, but how much untapped talent is available. If a student demonstrates a potential for benefiting from mediated learning experiences, then he or she is a suitable candidate for the program.

Instrumental Enrichment also has been used with students functioning at or above normal levels. However, Feuerstein himself seems unenthusiastic about this practice, except when the purpose is to correct some specific deficiency. The students who most need the program are those who are retarded performers. These include youngsters who have not had enough mediated learning experiences and those for whom these learning experiences, though provided, were not sufficient. (The latter include the congenitally retarded, the brain-damaged, the emotionally disturbed, and the physically handicapped.) No one suggests that the program is altogether wasted upon average and above-average students, but the program is essentially remedial and is therefore not right for all students.

Teacher Training and Qualifications

Nor is it right for all teachers. Feuerstein's theory about mediated learning experiences implies that the quality of interactions between teachers and their students is more important than the program exercises themselves.[8] And the art of providing mediated learning experiences is not easily acquired. J. McVicker Hunt, Emeritus Professor of Psychology at the University of Illinois and an enthusiastic supporter of Instrumental Enrichment, warns that administering the program "is a very, very hard thing to do. It takes brains, by God. You've got to work at it and you've got to think it through" (quoted in Chance, 1981, p. 73). Teachers must be intelligent and well-motivated if they are to succeed.

There are features of Instrumental Enrichment that also make it seem that those who implement the program should be clinical psychologists. While Feuerstein claims that ordinary teachers can learn to use the program, extensive training is required. In fact, one cannot readily obtain the course materials without having gone through a training program. Feuerstein believes that the minimum training for the program is an intensive two-week workshop. He also believes that an experienced consultant should be available to the teacher during his or her first two years of experience with the program. In the United States, such training and supervision are provided by Curriculum Developments Associates of Washington, D.C., and by the Western Center for Cognitive Education in California.

Evaluation

Is all the training and work worth the effort? Feuerstein himself clearly thinks so. He maintains that some pupils who started out as retarded performers have gone on to lead normal lives. For instance, "M" is the son of a psychotic and alcoholic father and a mentally retarded mother. Much of his childhood was spent in educationally and socially deprived environments. When he was referred for treatment at age 15, his IQ was between 35 and 45, and he had a vocabulary of forty to fifty words. After eleven years of intensive treatment, M speaks Hebrew and French and is responsible for the maintenance of a swimming pool. Instead of lifelong custodial care, he looks forward to "the life of an autonomous, independent, adaptive young man . . . " (Feuerstein, 1980, p. 10). Feuerstein offers numerous case studies of this sort in his books. Unfortunately, they do not make clear the role played by Instrumental Enrichment since other rehabilitative efforts are involved.[9]

More convincing, though less dramatic than these case studies, are anecdotes about the classroom use of Instrumental Enrichment with less severely disadvantaged students. Some of these suggest that students use their newfound skills outside of their Instrumental Enrichment classes. In one case, a teacher describes how a student applied what he had learned from the *Comparisons* exercises to a task in history class:

We were discussing Athens and Sparta, when suddenly one of my "weak" students spoke up: "Let's not do it this way. It isn't clear at all. Let's do it like we do in FIE [i.e., Feuerstein's Instrumental Enrichment]." I asked how he did it in FIE. He replied:

"We look for how they are alike and how they are different. There, we used things like color, size, number, direction. But that's not good here. We have to find the right dimensions on which we can compare Athens and Sparta." He then went to the blackboard, drew columns for Athens and Sparta, and asked for suggestions for the parameters for comparison, which he wrote on the side. "Now, it's clear and we can compare properly," he said. I must admit he was right. (Feuerstein, 1980, p. 278)

Other anecdotes suggest that students also apply Instrumental Enrichment skills in nonacademic situations. A physical-education teacher, for example, reported that one day a group of students, who were supposed to be playing volleyball, were engaged in a lively discussion about the organization and strategy of the team: Who should stand near the net? Who should play in the last row? Should the best players start or would it be better to put them in later? And so on. "This discussion was surprising enough," the teacher comments, "but the real shocker was that it was the culturally deprived kids who were doing the analyzing, thinking and planning" (Feuerstein, 1980, p. 142). The students involved were all taking Instrumental Enrichment.

As these examples imply, students (who often are skeptical at first) generally become enthusiastic about the exercises. Students are said to prefer the exercises to play, and those who are absent ask for work they have missed. Sometimes their enthusiasm for the program is excessive: Feuerstein (1980) tells of a young substitute teacher who reported to the school principal's office in tears after her students locked her out of the classroom saying, "Go tell the principal to send a substitute who knows Instrumental Enrichment" (p. 143).

Such anecdotal evidence is encouraging, but what about more formal research? Fewer studies have been done than one might expect, considering how long Instrumental Enrichment has been in use. One of the most extensive studies completed thus far was conducted by Feuerstein and Ya'acov Rand (1977; reported in Feuerstein, 1980). The study involved 218 Israeli adolescents, most of them male, with an average IQ of 80. Most of them came from low-income, blue-collar families. Many had records of poor school attendance and discipline problems; some had been in trouble with the police. Many were reading far below age level; some were almost illiterate. The experimental group received about three hundred hours of Instrumental Enrichment training over a two-year period; the control group spent the same time receiving supplementary academic instruction.

At the end of the training period, all students took a battery of intelligence tests. They also took four tests measuring more specific cognitive abilities. The researchers compared the scores of fifty-seven youths from each group matched for initial IQ, age, sex, and ethnic background. The results favored the Instrumental Enrichment group; the control group did not surpass the trained students on a single measure. A follow-up study conducted two years later suggested that the Instrumental Enrichment students maintained their advantage over the untrained students.

Other studies (e.g., Arbitman-Smith, Haywood, & Bransford, 1978) demonstrate that low-IQ students can, with training in one of the instruments, learn to perform as well on that kind of problem as do students with above-average IQs who have not had the training. Moreover, the training carries over to other kinds of tasks, such as to instruments the students have not seen before and even to everyday problems, such as planning for a field trip.

Such evidence has convinced some experts that Instrumental Enrichment can have powerful effects on some students (Bransford, Arbitman-Smith, Stein, and Vye, 1985; Sternberg, 1984). The question is whether what it does to those students justifies the problems the program brings with it. And there are problems.

One problem with Instrumental Enrichment is that it lacks what psychologists call face validity: Many of the instruments simply do not *look* as though they would teach useful thinking skills. It is likely that some parents and teachers will balk at the idea of having students spend part of the school day connecting dots, finding embedded figures, or creating designs by overlapping stencils.[10]

A related problem is the possibility that the skills taught may have limited applicability. Some psychologists have noted the similarity between items in the various instruments and items on IQ and aptitude tests. Does the program merely improve test-taking skills, or are the skills applicable to a wider range of tasks? Feuerstein believes that Instructional Enrichment increases what he calls "cognitive modifiability," the ability to benefit from experience.[11] If he is right, students who have had the training should learn more in their regular classes, and this should eventually show up on standardized achievement tests. There is, however, little evidence as yet to support this view.

Another problem with Instrumental Enrichment is that it requires a considerable investment of student time. Classes are held three to five times a week for two or three years, and there is evidence that there may be no sign of significant progress until after the first year. Feuerstein admits that the program does not produce immediate gains. In fact, he adds, "some students even become *less* efficient for a while, because they work more slowly, more thoughtfully."[12] This means that it is impossible to cut one's losses early on.

There also is a substantial investment of time and effort on the part of teachers. The program is not easily mastered, so teachers must spend a good deal of time reviewing lessons and improving their techniques. And since the program is to be continued for at least two years, more teachers must be trained than would be required for a shorter program.

Is Instrumental Enrichment worth all this trouble? Feuerstein likes to talk about the dramatic success stories: students who had functioned at the mildly retarded level and who are now attending college, working as librarians, holding important positions in business and government. No one would claim that the program brings about such dramatic results in all students, or even in most. But this may be a program that should not be evaluated in terms of average gains. Maybe we should evaluate Instrumental Enrichment in terms of the few dramatic success stories, the retarded performers who, as a result of training, go on to lead happy, fruitful lives. If so, the question becomes one of numbers: How many such successes are needed to justify implementation of the program? One in a hundred? One in a thousand? One in ten thousand? Whatever our answer may be, there can be no doubt about how that one child would answer.

7 Problem Solving and Comprehension

Arthur Whimbey traces his interest in teaching people how to think to his college days.

> I was interested in humor. I knew students who could thrust and parry with verbal swords with a facility that I could never match, and I wondered how they did it. One day I gave one of these students—I'll call him Ronald—an IQ test for a course I was taking. Ronald was a poor student, but he was very competent socially and very witty, so I was amazed when he earned an IQ score of about 75. I knew that Ronald was at least as bright as I was, and I began to wonder what he was doing wrong, and whether he could be taught to tackle problems more effectively.[1]

The experience with Ronald was like a brush with poison ivy: It caused an itch that demanded scratching.

Assumptions and Goals

On graduating from college, Whimbey went on to earn a Ph.D. in experimental psychology, and then took a teaching post at the University of Illinois. But the itch to understand people like Ronald persisted, and Whimbey soon found himself talking with the students who did poorly on the tests in his statistics courses. He asked them what they had done when working on a problem that they had solved incorrectly. "I found that they didn't do much of anything. They quickly read the problem and took a quick stab at the

PROBLEM SOLVING AND COMPREHENSION

Principal developer: Arthur Whimbey, Ph.D., independent educational consultant, Daytona Beach, Florida.

Assumptions: A few analytical skills are largely responsible for successful academic work. These skills can be imitated by poor students when demonstrated by experts.

Goals: To teach the kind of careful, systematic, analytical thinking characteristic of academically successful students.

Methods and materials: Students work in pairs on problems and then compare their efforts with model solutions. Usually offered as a one-semester course.

Audience: College freshmen and college-bound high school students. Intended primarily as a remedial program for students who are marginally qualified for college work.

Teacher qualifications: No special training or qualifications are considered necessary.

Benefits claimed: Students become more positive, more confident, more systematic in their approach to problems. Scores on academic aptitude tests improve.

Special problems: There is some question whether skills apply beyond tests. Vagueness of skills to be learned. Pair problem solving is unfamiliar to students.

Publisher: Franklin Institute Press, Box 2266, Philadelphia, PA 19103.

answer. They made no effort to tackle the problem in a systematic way."[2] Whimbey began to suspect that a student's success at solving test items, whether on an IQ test, a test in statistics, or a test in any other subject, had less to do with some innate ability than with the way the student attacked problems.

Whimbey decided to continue his work by offering intense tutoring to college students with poor academic skills. His method was to help the students work on the kinds of problems found on academic aptitude tests, such as the Scholastic Aptitude Test (SAT). For instance, while working on a reading comprehension item, the student would read the passage aloud, pausing after every sentence or two to explain to Whimbey exactly what the sentences meant. "Whenever a student had difficulty," Whimbey explains, "I asked questions, dropped hints, and in one way or another helped him to work out the meaning."[3] Once the student understood the passage, Whimbey had him read the first question aloud, interpret it, select an answer, and explain why that answer was correct. If, along the way, the student made an error, Whimbey pointed it out and explained why it was a mistake or asked questions to help the student see the error.

Whimbey noticed that sometimes students answered items incorrectly because of ignorance; they might, for instance, miss an analogy problem because they did not know the meaning of a word. And sometimes students failed because a problem involved subtle abstractions the student could not handle. But over and over again, Whimbey saw students miss items that did not require sophisticated information or involve abstract concepts. What impressed Whimbey about these low-scoring students was the way they thought when working on a problem.

Consider the example shown in figure 5. Four figures form a series that changes according to some rule. The task is to discover the rule and choose the figure that should occur next in the series. One college student chose alternative *E* and gave this explanation:

> First there are some lines taken away. Then there are more lines taken away going the other way. Then there are more lines taken away going up and down. So I guess the answer should be take away more lines. I guess answer 'E.' (Whimbey, 1976, p. 29)

Figure 5. A problem used by Whimbey to study thinking.

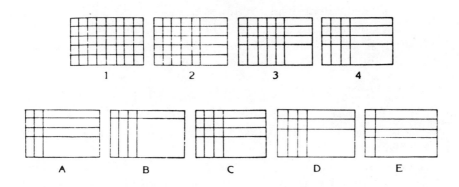

When successful students work on this problem, they make the same observation as the poor student: Some lines are taken away. But the good students do not stop there; they go on to count the number of lines missing from each square (perhaps writing them down on the page) and deduce the pattern: Take away two vertical lines, then take away one horizontal line. Once they discover the pattern, they have only to count the number of lines in each alternate square to find the right answer.

Here is another problem, along with the analysis of a weak student:

> If you have three boxes, and inside each box there are two smaller boxes, and inside each of these boxes there are four even smaller boxes, how many boxes are there altogether?
>   A)24   B)12   C)13   D)21   E)33   F)36
>
> I pictured the three boxes and the two smaller boxes inside the three boxes . . . I added three plus two (which is five) and counted the four other boxes twice. Five plus eight gave me 13. (Whimbey, 1976, p. 29)

The correct answer is easily derived by the student who sketches little boxes and then counts them. This is not a technique that requires great talent; it just requires doing.

Drawing upon his experience and the handful of related studies in the research literature, Whimbey identified five characteristics that distinguish successful students from unsuccessful ones:

1. POSITIVE ATTITUDE. Successful students believe that problems can be solved through careful, persistent analysis. In contrast, less successful students take the view that "either you know it or you don't."
2. CONCERN FOR ACCURACY. Strong students are careful. They reread sentences they do not understand, check their arithmetic, make sure they have done what the problem asks, and so on. Weak students are slipshod. They dash through a problem without regard for detail or precision.
3. BREAKING THE PROBLEM INTO PARTS. Good students have learned that a complex problem can be broken down into a number of simpler problems, and that each of these can be solved in turn to reach a solution. Poor students, on the other hand, attempt to solve complex problems in one fell swoop.
4. AVOIDANCE OF GUESSING. Successful students work all the way through a problem until they reach a solution. If they run into trouble, they find a way of overcoming it. Unsuccessful students have a penchant for guessing, especially when they run into trouble.
5. ACTIVENESS IN PROBLEM SOLVING. Good students do lots of things when working on a problem: They talk to themselves; count on their fingers; draw sketches, diagrams, or tables; and circle or underline important words in a question and so on. Poor students do not.[4]

In short, good students approach problems in a methodical, systematic, analytical manner that is foreign to poor students. Yet for the most part, successful students do nothing that is beyond the *capacity* of their less successful peers. The question is how to teach poor students to do the same sort of things good students do. Whimbey's answer to this question (prepared with the help of Jack Lochhead of the University of Massachusetts) was *Problem Solving and Comprehension* (Whimbey and Lochhead, 1982).

Methods and Materials

Problem Solving and Comprehension is both text and workbook for a course in thinking. The course is usually given over one semester. It begins with students taking the Whimbey Analytical Skills Inventory (WASI). The WASI is similar to standardized intelligence and aptitude tests, and students take it in order to achieve some insight into their own thinking. After taking the test, the students spend several days going over it item by item. They take turns explaining how they attempted to solve a problem and comparing their methods with those of their classmates. The object is to help the students see the kinds of mistakes they make in tackling problems.

In chapter two, selected WASI items are analyzed, and common errors are pointed out along with ways of avoiding them. For instance, item 10 of the WASI is a simple math problem:

> Ten full crates of walnuts weigh 410 lb, while an empty crate weighs 10 lb. How much do the walnuts alone weigh? (Whimbey and Lochhead, 1982, p. 13)

Whimbey and Lochhead explain that, while many people panic at the sight of such problems, if you look at the problem closely, "you see that it doesn't require any mysterious ability. All that this problem demands is that the facts be spelled out fully and accurately. Once that is done, the remaining arithmetic is simple" (p. 13). The text then shows how sketching a simple diagram will help the student spell out the facts.

Chapter three builds on this foundation by developing further the idea that analytical thinking is a learned skill. Topics covered include the hidden nature of thinking, the consequent need for thinking aloud, and the need for demonstration and guided practice to develop skill at thinking. The students are then given two demonstrations of skilled problem solving in the form of the protocol of an expert problem solver who thinks aloud as he works. Here is one problem and its model solution:

> [Problem solver reads aloud,] "If the word *sentence* contains less than 9 letters and more than 3 vowels, circle the first vowel. Otherwise circle the consonant which is farthest to the right in the word."

I'll start from the beginning.

[Reads] "If the word *sentence* contains less than 9 letters."

I'll count the letters in *sentence*. [Points to letters while counting] 1, 2, 3, 4, 5, 6, 7, 8. Let me check it. 1, 2, 3, 4, 5, 6, 7, 8. So it does have less than 9 letters. I'll write *yes* above the problem. That way I'll remember it. [Writes *yes* over problem.]

"And more than 3 vowels."

[Points while counting] 1, 2, 3. Let me check that. 1, 2, 3. It contains exactly 3 vowels, not more than 3 vowels. I'll write *no* on the problem to remind me.

"Circle the first vowel."

So I won't do that.

"Otherwise circle the consonant which is farthest to the right in the word."

The consonant farthest to the right? Let me see. Which is my right hand. This is my right hand. OK, so the last letter is the one farthest to the right. But the last letter is *E*. The next letter over is *C*. So it is the consonant farthest to the right. I'll circle the *C*. (p. 25)

This and another demonstration illustrate the five character-istics of good students. These characteristics are reviewed for the students, who are then ready to begin tackling problems themselves. Or, rather, they are almost ready. Demonstration, according to Whimbey, is a vital part of skill learning, but it is not the whole of it. Another essential is *informed* practice. Ideally, students should receive feedback from an expert problem solver, but it is not possible to assign one to each student taking the course. How, then, are the students to get the feedback they need to improve their problem-solving efforts? Whimbey's answer is pair problem solving.

In pair problem solving, two students work together, alternately taking the role of problem solver and listener. The problem solver thinks aloud as he works, explaining every step he takes toward a solution to a problem. The listener does two things: She constantly demands that the problem solver think aloud, and she points out errors. The listener works along with the problem solver, following every step the latter takes. The listener must never let the problem solver get ahead of her and may have to ask the problem solver to wait a moment while she checks the accuracy of a calculation or the validity of a conclusion. However, the listener must avoid the tendency to work on the problem independently or to give the problem solver hints. The listener's job is not to solve the problem but to catch errors made by the problem solver.

The idea behind prompting the problem solver to think aloud is to get the normally hidden activity of thinking out in the open, where both the listener and the problem solver can better observe it. Pointing out errors provides the informed feedback needed to improve performance. Whimbey feels that both problem solver and listener learn during pair problem solving.

Once the pair problem-solving procedure has been explained and demonstrated, the students begin using it on problems. The program provides practice in four kinds of problems: verbal reasoning, analogies, trend analysis, and mathematical word problems. In each case there is a brief introduction to the nature of the problems, followed by two sets of practice items. In the first set, each practice problem is followed by a model solution illustrating the steps to be taken in working the problem successfully. If the problem solver's answer to one of these problems is incorrect, both students study the model solution provided. They also take note of any problem-solving aids or strategies (diagrams, tables, figures, etc.) demonstrated. In the second set of problems, the answers are provided, but not the steps necessary to reach the answers. The items in each practice set represent something of a progression, with the easiest problems coming first.

Chapter four treats verbal reasoning problems such as, "Paul and Tom are the same age. Paul is older than Cynthia. Cynthia is younger than Hal. Is Paul older or younger than Hal—or can this not be determined from the information?" (p. 47).

There are forty problems of this sort, with demonstrated solutions, followed by forty-two items for which answers, but not model solutions, are provided.[5]

The chapter on verbal reasoning problems is followed by a short chapter on reading. There are no problems to be worked; the unit is really a critique of speed reading. Students are advised to break many of the rules promulgated by advocates of speed reading. Whimbey tells students they *should* read every word, subvocalize, and reread sentences they do not understand. "If you want to master your academic subjects and perform well on tests," students are told, "you must read with care and thoroughness, and give the work the time it requires. There are no magical shortcuts" (p. 140).

The next three chapters of the text deal with analogy problems. In chapter six the student learns how to use relationship sentences in solving these problems. For instance, the analogy, "*Gills* are related to *fish* as *lungs* are related to *humans*," can be represented by the relationship sentence, "_____ are used for breathing by _____" (p. 143). The student then gets practice in selecting appropriate relationship sentences—that is, in selecting the sentence that correctly describes an analogy. This work is followed in chapter seven with practice at writing relationship sentences. Then in chapter eight the students solve analogy problems such as

Thermometer is to temperature as _____ is to _____.
a. telescope : astronomy   c. scale : weight
b. clock : minutes   d. microscope : biologist (p. 171)

In chapter nine, the students turn their attention to problems involving trends and patterns. Here the task is to discover the pattern in a series, such as 3, 6, 9, 12 or A, C, E, G, and predict the next items in the series.

The tenth chapter treats mathematical word problems such as, "A certain ruler, which is supposed to be 12 inches long, is warped and is actually just 11½ inches. If you measure off 4 feet of string with this ruler, how long will the string really be?" (p. 233). The final chapter of the text offers the students another test, the Post-WASI, so that they can see how much the course has improved their thinking.

Throughout the course, students work together in pairs and then study the model solution. Whimbey notes that model solutions are provided not merely to show the student the correct answers but to demonstrate the characteristics of analytical thinking. To emphasize this point, Whimbey occasionally illustrates two different ways of solving a given problem. For instance, consider this trend analysis problem: "2 7 4 9 6 11 8 13 __ __ __" (p. 199). One way of analyzing this series leads to the pattern of alternately adding 5 and subtracting 3. But it also is possible to think of the problem as two series of numbers: 2 4 6 8 and 7 9 11 13. Viewed this way, the pattern becomes two alternating series of numbers, each increasing by two. Both analyses yield the same answer.

For the most part, the program relies upon solution demonstrations in the text and pair problem-solving experiences to improve student performance. However, from time to time the students are given additional hints about how to go about solving a particular kind of problem. For instance, students learn that a common error in solving analogy problems is to select an answer that reverses the direction of the relationship. In the analogy, 2 is to 6 as __ is to __ , students sometimes select the answer, 3 : 1. But this reverses, rather than matches, the relationship in the first pair and is therefore incorrect. Students also learn to use Venn diagrams and other techniques for representing problem statements graphically, and they learn to talk to themselves (even when no listener is present) about the problem and what they are doing to solve it. Throughout the course the students are reminded of the importance of being positive, looking out for errors, and displaying other characteristics of successful students.

In addition to the pair problem-solving work in class, students may be given homework to do on their own. This consists of making up problems of the type being studied and then having another student solve them, thinking aloud as he does so. Having students invent problems in this way is intended to help them see problems "from the inside out" (p. 39f).

Target Audience

Problem Solving and Comprehension is intended for use with young adults with poor academic skills. Some students who take the course are interested primarily in improving scores on a screening test, such as the Scholastic Aptitude Test. Others hope that it will improve their grades. In general, these students have total SAT scores below 800 (about a hundred points below the current average). However, Whimbey believes that many students with SATs of 1000 or even 1200 might benefit from the program. The text is most often used with entering college students and college-bound high school students, especially those with marginal qualifications for college work.

However, there would seem to be no reason for excluding secondary-school students of average or even below-average ability. Of course, students can go through the text alone, rather than with a class. However, this means sacrificing the benefits of pair problem solving and the support of an instructor.

Teacher Training and Qualifications

Support, incidentally, is just about all the instructor needs to provide. Most of the benefits from the course come from reading the text and doing pair problem solving. The instructor's chief responsibilities seem to be those of introducing the course, leading the class discussion of the WASI, and providing moral support to students whose progress is slow. During pair problem solving, the teacher monitors the students to ensure that they are performing their roles properly. However, the teacher is supposed to avoid putting the students in a passive role. For example, questions are to be met with questions, not answers. The teacher's role, then, is rather like that of the listener in pair problem solving.[6] Consequently, no special teacher training is deemed necessary, though Whimbey does sometimes offer workshops at schools where the program is to be offered.

Evaluation

One question those attending these workshops are likely to ask is whether the students who go through the program will learn how to think analytically or merely how to answer test questions. Whimbey leaves no doubt about his answer. He considers the problems included in the program a means of developing the skills needed for all academic work. For example, in justifying the work on analogy problems he tells his students, "As you work the analogy problems in the chapter, you will find it necessary to spell ideas out fully, formulate precise relationships of facts, seek correspondences between diverse ideas, and compare relationships for similarities and differences. *These are the activities which underlie the mastery of all academic courses, stretching from poetry to political science to calculus"* (Whimbey & Lochhead, 1982, p. 142f; emphasis added). So the theory goes. But what is the evidence?

Actually, there is not much evidence, one way or the other. Whimbey and others who have used the program believe that they have seen positive results. Whimbey offers some impressive case-study evidence for his methods in his book, *Intelligence Can Be Taught* (1975). For example, he tells of a student who scored 385 on the Law Scholastic Aptitude Test (LSAT) and 750 on the Graduate Record Exam (GRE). At this point the student began working with Whimbey two hours a day, four days a week. After eight weeks of tutoring, the student retook the LSAT and scored 432, a gain of nearly fifty points. After a few more weeks of work he retook the GRE and scored 820. After this, the student discontinued the lessons, but in six months he tried the GRE a third time and this time scored 890—a gain of 140 points over his initial score. However, such case studies illustrate the effects of intensive individual tutoring, not the classroom use of *Problem Solving and Comprehension*, so the results are difficult to interpret.

Some instructors who have used the program have reported good results. The director of a project at Manhattan Community College in New York reports that students who took the course became more effective in their regular classes. These observations were consistent with the reactions of the students themselves, who said that they were using their new skills in their schoolwork (Hutchinson, 1985).

Jack Lochhead, who collaborated with Whimbey on *Problem Solving and Comprehension*, has used the text at the University of Massachusetts. He believes that the major effects of the program are delayed. "We don't see remarkable changes in the students by the end of the course," he says, "but we think that the course gets them started toward a more analytical approach."[7] This is reflected, Lochhead believes, in higher overall grade-point averages across the four-year college program and in higher graduation rates among those who have taken the course.

Although *Problem Solving and Comprehension* was intended as a course in analytical thinking, it has been put to another use. Some instructors in certain content areas, especially English and reading, have used it to help their students acquire analytical skills they can apply to the course content. In these instances, the instructor typically spends the first two or three weeks going through *Problem Solving and Comprehension* (skipping many of the practice items), and then turns to the standard curriculum. In some cases the instructor continues the use of pair problem solving, but has the students apply it to the solution of algebra or physics problems, as the case may be.

There is as yet little experimental evidence of the program's effectiveness. Apparently only two research studies have been reported, and in neither case was the course offered strictly as Whimbey intended. At Bloomfield College in New Jersey, two remedial math courses were redesigned to include *Problem Solving and Comprehension*, while two other classes were taught by the conventional method (Sadler and Whimbey, 1980). At the end of the semester, average class improvements on a post-test revealed a substantial advantage for those students whose work included Whimbey's course. The students taking the conventional course showed a gain of just under a year in mathematical proficiency, while those taking the redesigned course gained an average of three years.

At Xavier University of Louisiana, the text is part of a remedial summer program for entering freshmen. This program reportedly produces average gains on the Preliminary Scholastic Aptitude Test (the PSAT is a standardized test used to prepare students for the SAT) of about eighty-five points. J. W. Carmichael, director of the program, says that gains of two hundred or more points on the PSAT are fairly common.[8] Unfortunately, since *Problem Solving and Comprehension* is only part of a complex program aimed at improving the academic skills of Xavier students, it is impossible to know to what extent Whimbey's program is responsible for these gains. Carmichael nevertheless feels certain that the text plays an important role in the success of the Xavier program.

Thus, while there is a dearth of hard data, there is evidence that suggests that the program can produce substantial improvements in the analytical skills of poorly prepared college-bound students. Now for the problems encountered on the way to those improvements.

One problem with the program is the vagueness of some of the skills to be learned. Whimbey stresses the similarity between learning to think analytically and learning to play tennis, for example. But the skills of tennis can be reduced to specific kinds of behavior (foot placement, racket grip, ball toss, and so on), while the skills of analytical thinking identified by Whimbey do not have this same sort of concreteness. It is true, for instance, that good problem solvers approach problems with a positive attitude, but what exactly does having a positive attitude entail?

Another problem concerns pair problem solving. Both the problem solver and the listener roles require some learning. Students who are not accustomed to carrying on a silent dialogue with themselves as they work on a problem (and this is true of many of the less successful students) are apt to have trouble thinking aloud. And listeners are apt to get wrapped up in the problem themselves and forget that their function is to monitor the behavior of the problem solver. Pair problem solving, as Whimbey describes it, is *not* the sort of collaborative effort in which students customarily engage when studying together. Whimbey admits that it takes time to get used to this procedure, but he maintains that with a bit of practice most students become proficient at it.

Finally, there are a number of unanswered questions about the program. Should the students engaged in pair problem solving be matched for ability? Do students learn more in their role as listener or while acting as problem solver? Can students who are not good problem solvers be effective listeners? Should instructors go over problems in class after the students have worked on them? How many problems of a given type do students need to do? The teacher's guide provides little help in answering such questions.

Still, the program seems quite straightforward, and it is easy to believe that most instructors will be able to answer most of the questions that arise to their own satisfaction. Whether the program produces enough improvement in students to justify its continuance is one question the teacher will have to answer. As for that, Whimbey reminds us that expertise at thinking, like expertise at anything else, requires many hours of study and practice. This is a one-semester program involving perhaps forty hours of study and practice.[9] Whimbey points out that if students were to spend a similar amount of time learning golf, they would not expect to be ready for the professional golfing tour. They would hope only to have acquired the fundamentals. All that Whimbey hopes his students will acquire from a semester spent on his course is the fundamentals of analytical thinking. It has to be admitted that if the course achieves even this modest goal, it must be judged a remarkable success.

8 Techniques of Learning

Donald Dansereau had done well in high school, so he was a little surprised to find himself faltering in his first semester at the State University of New York at Buffalo. "In high school," he explains, "I just ground away at the books, reading and rereading them until I had the material down pat. But in college, that didn't work. There was just too much material."[1] In his second semester, Dansereau tried a new approach. He spent less time rereading the books and more time thinking about their contents. The plan worked. "My grades went up and the amount of time I spent studying went down."[2]

Curiously, Dansereau's new approach to academics may have come from something he learned in sports.

> I was very active in sports in college, but I relied almost entirely on brute strength. When I threw the discus, for example, I just concentrated on throwing it as hard as I could. Gradually, I came to realize the value of technique, and I applied that same insight to my studies. I learned that it isn't just intense effort that gets you where you want to go; technique is important too.[3]

Assumptions and Goals

Dansereau's mastery of learning techniques was good enough to win him an award in his junior year as the most promising engineering student in the university. In his last year of college, however, Dansereau's interest in engineering waned and he went on to earn a Ph.D. in psychology at the Carnegie Institute of Technology. There he studied how students solve difficult problems in

TECHNIQUES OF LEARNING

Principal developer: Donald Dansereau, Ph.D., Professor of Psychology, Texas Christian University.

Assumptions: Academic success is a function of the kinds of thinking students do when attempting to learn, recall, and use information. Technique is more important than effort.

Goals: To teach students effective, easy-to-use techniques for mastering academic information, especially in texts.

Methods and materials: Offered as a one-semester course consisting of seven units. Each unit explains, demonstrates, and provides practice in the use of one or more techniques.

Audience: Offered primarily to college students, but some modules may be suitable for use with high school students.

Teacher qualifications: No special training or qualifications required. Some workshops available.

Benefits claimed: Improves performance on teacher-made tests. Students spend less time studying yet get better grades in regular classes.

Special problems: Materials are not commercially available; units not well integrated; no teacher's guide.

Publisher: Not in print. Sample modules are available from Dansereau at Texas Christian University, Fort Worth, TX 76129.

mental arithmetic, such as multiplying 702,865 times 43. The students thought out loud as they worked, and Dansereau recorded their efforts. He found that there were wide differences among the students in the ability to perform such tasks, and that these differences were due to two factors. One was special knowledge. The more a person knew about numbers and their relationships, the more rapidly he could solve a problem. Some students knew, for example, that 11 times 12 is 132, which meant that they did not have to work out this bit of arithmetic in their heads. The second important component was technique. The really proficient students used all sorts of strategies to get them through. For instance, if asked to multiply 72 by 49, the best students might begin by multiplying 70 times 40, then add to that the products of 9 times 70 and 2 times 49. Such strategies may seem cumbersome, but to the person who is well-practiced in their use, they greatly simplify the problem. Once again Dansereau saw that technique played a powerful role in the performance of academic tasks.

Dansereau moved on to Texas Christian University where he continued to study learning techniques under grants from the National Institute of Education and other agencies. Again and again he found that when students used certain techniques, their learning improved.[4] Some of these techniques, which he came to call "primary strategies," help the students directly in mastering texts by improving comprehension or recall. Other techniques, called "support strategies," help indirectly by improving the student's ability to concentrate or by reducing anxiety. Dansereau reasoned that if such individual techniques enhanced academic performance, an *interactive system* of techniques should be especially useful. His efforts to design such a system of techniques resulted in a program that will be called here Techniques of Learning.[5]

The Techniques of Learning program has been offered at Texas Christian University since 1976, but the course continues to undergo revision. Dansereau looks upon the program the way a mechanical engineer looks upon a drill press.

What I do in perfecting the course is basically what engineers do in perfecting machinery. They take a machine apart and test its various components. These detailed analyses lead them to discover weaknesses and to see areas for improvement that they couldn't possibly have discovered by testing the intact machine. They then modify the components accordingly, and put them back into the machine to see how it functions. In our case, the 'machine' is the course and the 'components' are units for teaching the various techniques.[6]

Methods and Materials

The course consists of a series of seven units, each intended to teach a particular technique or set of techniques. In general, a unit consists of a series of mimeographed booklets that explain the technique to be learned, demonstrate its use, and provide practice exercises.[7] The instructor does some lecturing, answers questions, and demonstrates the correct use of the techniques, but most class time is spent reading the booklets and working on exercises. Sometimes the students work on the exercises in pairs, with one student thinking out loud as he works on the material and the other one making comments and correcting errors the learner makes.[8] After class, the students may have a homework assignment such as practicing a technique on a chapter of one of their regular textbooks.

The first unit introduces the students to an overall technique for academic success. This "metastrategy" (a strategy for implementing strategies) guides the students through each step of the process of learning. Dansereau has a penchant for acronyms, and he has managed to wrestle the steps of this metastrategy into the acronym MURDER:

MOOD. The first step in studying is to get into the right mood, to free oneself of negative feelings.

UNDERSTANDING. This step involves reading for understanding. Students learn not to get bogged down in details but to read for the main ideas.

RECALL. Students close their books and recall as much of the material as they can.

DIGEST. The students open the text again and check their recall.

EXPAND KNOWLEDGE. Students ask themselves questions about the material and then search for the answers.

REVIEW. Students go over their classroom tests to find out what mistakes they made and why.[9]

Each of the six steps in the metastrategy is explained in more detail. For example, in the "understand" stage, the students are to read short sections of a chapter. As they read, they are to mark difficult passages and important ideas. They also are encouraged to read actively—that is, to form mental images of the material, to make jokes, and so on. Similarly, students learn that in digesting the material they should pay special attention to points that they were unable to recall. As you will see, the units that follow MURDER build upon this metastrategy.

Unit two deals with the M of MURDER by teaching the students various techniques for creating and maintaining a good mood.[10] By far the greatest attention in this unit is given to a technique called positive self-talk. Dansereau believes that mood is affected by the kinds of things people say to themselves (usually covertly). If students say negative, defeatist kinds of things, they are in a negative, defeatist mood—and will have a tendency to turn to something that will improve their mood, such as chatting with friends. If students say positive things to themselves, their mood improves, and they are able to focus their attention on learning.

Students learn to talk positively to themselves by reading typical negative comments (the sort of rationalizing and self-deprecating things students often hear themselves saying), and then attempting to rebut these statements with positive comments. They are then shown a demonstration of what they might have said. For instance, one item consists of a familiar rationalization for not studying: "I've only got forty-five minutes 'til I have to be somewhere. That's really not enough time to study." The student writes out a challenge to this statement and then reads the following model challenge: "Oops! I use that excuse a lot! I suppose I could at least get started and get a feel for how much there is to read. Besides, I'm always on my way somewhere except at night and I'm really tired then (Dansereau, 1978b, p. 4).

The third unit in the course teaches students how to use schemas for identifying and organizing what they must learn in a course. "One of the best and easiest ways of improving your grades," reads the introduction, "is to learn how . . . teachers think about their subject matter" (p. 1). There are certain kinds of topics students study in their courses: theories, events, systems, techniques, objects, and concepts. For instance, the biology teacher who makes up a test is apt to include questions on theories, such as Darwin's theory of evolution; events, such as the discovery of penicillin; systems, such as the circulatory system; techniques, such as naturalistic observation; objects, such as protozoa; and concepts, such as spermatogenesis. But what are the students expected to know about such topics? This unit helps the students answer this question by providing them with schemas for the kinds of things teachers are likely to expect them to know. These schemas are reduced to acronyms so that they are easy to recall. For instance, students learn that DICEOX tells them the kinds of things they must know about a theory:

DESCRIBE. What is the theory about? What does it say?

INVENTOR. Who is credited with having invented the theory?

CONSEQUENCES. What effects or implications does the theory have?

EVIDENCE. What is the evidence for the theory?

OTHER THEORIES. What competing theories are there? How do they differ from the one under consideration?

XTRA. What other points are important?

DICEOX answers the question, What do I need to know about this theory? The student can go through the DICEOX questions when studying a theory in order to focus attention on key points. The acronym also serves as a way of prompting recall of the theory. This can come in handy when answering essay questions such as, "Compare the theory of evolution with creationism."

The use of DICEOX is demonstrated on the theory of evolution, and then the student is asked to use the technique to recall information about the theory of gravity. After this, the students compare their efforts against a model. This feedback helps them evaluate the adequacy of their own efforts.

After DICEOX, the students take up DACO, which identifies the kinds of information to be learned about events: Description, Antecedents, Consequences, and Other related events. The use of DACO is demonstrated and practiced in the same way as DICEOX. After DACO the students learn schemas that will help them master, in turn, systems, techniques, and objects. Each schema-acronym is introduced, demonstrated, and practiced.

Unit four teaches students how to organize text material so that it is easier to understand and remember. The student learns that the first thing to do with a chapter (even before reading it) is to use the headings to make a set of skeleton maps. The students are advised to make a map of an entire chapter using the major section headings and then to make separate maps for each of these sections using the author's subheadings.

After a brief explanation, the students skim a short passage and then study a map of the passage constructed from its headings. After this, the students make their own map of a second passage, a composition on the human nervous system and biofeedback. They then compare their maps of the passage with one prepared by Dansereau. The next step consists of practicing mapping on a textbook. These maps are brought to class so that the instructor can provide feedback.

The longest, most extensive unit, the fifth, is devoted to networking, a technique for filling in the chapter maps.[11] In networking the student identifies the important ideas in each section or subsection of a chapter and represents them in a kind of outline. To this extent, networking is simply detailed mapping. But the emphasis in networking is not on the ideas extracted from a text, but on their relationships to one another. The real object of networking is to enhance understanding by seeing how ideas are connected. The first step in learning to network is, therefore, learning to identify the various kinds of relationships, or links, that tie ideas together. Dansereau identifies six kinds of links:

PART OF—Fingers are part of the hand.
TYPE OF—An ant is a type of insect.
LEAD TO—Practice leads to perfection.
ANALOGY—An eye is like a camera.
CHARACTERISTIC—Pinocchio is characterized by a wooden body.
EVIDENCE—A broken arm is evidence of an accident.

The students receive practice in identifying the various kinds of links. For example, they are asked to identify the link (or connection) between the words *disease* and *pneumonia*. As always, the correct answers are provided (pneumonia is a *type of* disease) so that the students know right away when they have missed a beat. After this the students network individual sentences, then a series of sentences, and finally whole paragraphs.

Next the students learn that paragraphs and large bodies of text usually have a main structure around which the ideas are organized. If they can identify this structure, they can use it to identify the links among the ideas. Dansereau suggests that there are three types of link structures (see figure 6). Hierarchical structures involve "part of" or "type of" links; chain structures use "lead to" links; and spider structures have links that are "analogies," "characteristics," or "evidence."

Paragraph networking is demonstrated on a short, simple paragraph about igneous rocks. After this the students work on three practice paragraphs, with each effort followed by a model network to provide feedback. While the main structure of a paragraph is a hierarchy, a chain, or a spider, more than one type of structure may be needed to network a paragraph in detail.

The final stage in network training explains how to combine mapping and networking when studying a chapter in a text. The students are instructed to begin by making an overview map using the author's headings. Second, they should read the passage, marking important ideas. Third, they should fill in the maps by networking. Finally, they should read the completed maps to make sure they capture the author's meaning. After this review, the students practice the procedure on chapter summaries and other material.

The sixth unit is on techniques intended to help the students prepare for classroom tests. The first of these techniques is map-assessment; it consists of evaluating the completed maps of a chapter. This is done by using the schemas learned in unit three. For instance, the students identify all the theories that appear in the maps, and then go through the DICEOX checklist to ensure that the maps contain all the necessary information about each theory. When this has been done for the theories, the students go through their maps and pick out every event, then use the DACO acronym to ensure that they have all the pertinent information for each event. After this has been done for the events, a like procedure is followed for systems, techniques, objects, and concepts in the chapter.

Figure 6. Networking three kinds of link structures.

1. (HIERARCHIES)

    a. [PART] Hierarchy

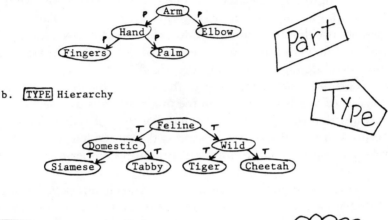

    b. [TYPE] Hierarchy

2. (CHAINS)   Leads to Chains

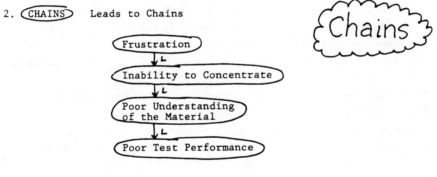

3. (SPIDERS)   Analogy, Characteristic, Evidence

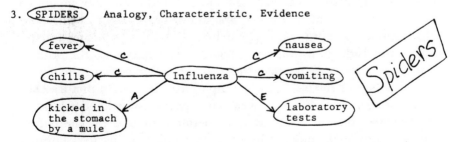

Reprinted from unit five of Techniques of Learning by permission of Donald Dansereau.

After this description of map-assessment, the students are shown a demonstration of the techniques applied to one of the passages covered in the first unit. Then they practice the technique on the second passage from that unit. When map-assessment is complete, and the maps appropriately modified, the students know what they have to know about a chapter to do well on a test. The next step is to be sure that they know it. Toward this end, Dansereau provides training in various memory techniques. Each one is, of course, described, demonstrated, and practiced.

The first aid to memory is the numbering technique, which consists of numbering items on the maps. It helps, Dansereau writes, to know that there are three branches of the U.S. government when trying to recall them. Numbering is demonstrated on the map for one passage; then the students practice numbering on another passage.

After the items to be recalled have been numbered, they can be rehearsed. Most students rehearse by repeating the material over and over, but Dansereau recommends rehearsing facts in a form that suggests a test question such as, "The circulatory system has two major functions, (1) _____ and (2)_____" or "Man has five senses, (1)_____ (2)_____ (3)_____ (4)_____ and (5)_____" (Dansereau, 1978d, p. 2).

Dansereau also recommends inventing acronyms. For example, JEL would help a student remember the judicial, executive, and legislative branches of our government.

To remember lists of items too long for acronyms, Dansereau recommends either of two mnemonic systems. In the "peg word" system, the student memorizes a list of peg words, one for each of a certain number of integers. The pegs should be easily imagined real objects, not abstractions, and they should rhyme with their corresponding number (one is a bun, two is a shoe, and so on). Once this is done, the students "hang" information on the pegs by forming images that connect them. If the task is to learn the names of a number of scientists, for example, students might picture Darwin eating a bun, Einstein wearing a pair of weird shoes, and so on. In the "mental walk" system (better known as the method of loci) the student "places" items at particular points in a familiar area, such as a house or a frequently traveled path. When the time comes to recall the items, the student takes an imaginary walk in the area and "sees" what objects are there.

Once students have prepared for a test, their next task is to take it. The last unit offers guidelines on how to take tests more effectively. These guidelines are actually test-taking techniques. They will not, of course, provide answers to questions on material the student has not studied. They will, however, help students do their best on material they have studied. The unit begins with a three-step procedure for taking tests:

1. SET THE MOOD. Students are told that before they take any test they should always attempt to set an appropriate mood. Being in an appropriate mood means being relaxed, positive, and free of thoughts unrelated to the test. "You can set a good mood," students learn, "by taking a minute to imagine yourself going through the test like a cool, confident, professional student" (Dansereau, 1978c, p. 1).

2. UNDERSTAND. "Your next step," the student reads, "is to *understand* what kind of information the teacher is looking for" (Dansereau, 1978c, p. 2). To do this, the students are to read through the entire test. As they do so, they answer the easy questions and circle or underline important words or phrases (*not, describe briefly,* and so forth), cross out obviously incorrect alternatives on multiple-choice items, jot down points to cover in answering essay questions, and note in the margins the numbers of related questions.

3. REREAD. The third step is to go through the test again, rereading the unanswered questions and trying to determine why these questions are hard. Is an item difficult because the student does not understand what is wanted? If so, it may help to study related items (noted earlier; see above) for hints about what is wanted. Sometimes the confusion stems from a particular word, such as *describe* or *compare.* In these instances, the student is advised to recall how the teacher used those terms in class. What does the teacher do when giving a description or when comparing two things? Sometimes the meaning of a test item is perfectly clear; its difficulty derives from the student's inability to recall the answer. In this event, the student should try to recall related

information. This can be done by reconstructing a network of the material.

This three-step procedure is intended primarily for short-answer and multiple-choice tests. What about essay tests? To write better essays, Dansereau suggests a five-step procedure that begins with networking the material to be covered. As in the other units, the test-taking unit includes demonstrations of the various techniques. For example, after the essay-writing technique is described, the student is shown an essay question, a network of the relevant information, and the final essay.

Target Audience

The Techniques of Learning course just summarized is open to all students at Texas Christian University, and is taken by a cross section of them. However, some of the course materials have been used in other settings with different audiences. The United States Air Force has used some of the materials in preparing enlisted personnel for technical schools. And some of the units have been used with high school students. Thus, while the course was designed for students at TCU, Dansereau believes that the materials could be adapted for use in a number of different settings and with different kinds of students. However, since many of the best students in high school and college already use the strategies taught by the course, the program is of greatest value to weaker students.

Teacher Training and Qualifications

The course units are designed to be largely self-instructional, so special teacher training is not considered necessary. Student motivation is far more important than instructional style, Dansereau says, so the teacher's main job is to convince the students that the techniques really will help them. "Once the students see that a technique works," he explains, "they'll master it. The trouble is that learning to use the techniques effectively is often slow, hard work. At first the techniques are cumbersome and time-consuming.

The students need to be convinced that they will pay off in the end."[12]

Though Dansereau offers no formal teacher training for those who might like to adopt the course, he does give workshops in which he demonstrates how the units are used. "The best instruction in teaching the units is to go through the units as a student would and use the techniques," says Dansereau. "This will enable the teacher to help students who are having problems with a technique."[13] Thus, in his workshops, he has potential teachers go through some of the course units.

Evaluation

Dansereau believes that the teachers who use his units can expect to find the students receptive. TCU students who have had the course routinely report that they find the techniques useful and use them in their other classes. And some students who have had the course some months before come back to tell Dansereau that they spend less time studying yet get better grades.

Such comments are heartening to any teacher, but Dansereau admits that they provide only shaky support for the program. Stronger support is available in the form of experimental studies of the individual units. In one study, Dansereau and his coworkers (Holley, Dansereau, McDonald, Garland, & Collins, 1979) examined the value of networking. Seventeen college students received about six hours of training in networking, using materials similar to those described earlier. The students then used networking to study a three-thousand-word passage from a geology text. Five days later they took a series of tests on this passage. A comparable group of students also studied the passage using their normal study methods and, five days later, took the same tests. Overall, those trained in networking did better on the tests than did the control students. Training had no effect on questions about details, but a very substantial effect on questions about main ideas. The untrained students answered an average of 47 percent of such questions correctly, while the trained students averaged 63 percent.

Similar studies have assessed the effectiveness of mapping, positive self-talk, and other techniques taught in the course. Dansereau

(1985) reports that these studies typically show that the individual techniques result in the students' learning, on average, 30 to 40 percent more than students who are left to their own devices. In other words, if the average untrained student answers 65 percent of the items on a test correctly, the average trained student is likely to get about 85 percent right. That is the difference between a D and a B, a difference most students and teachers would consider noteworthy.

Of course, students who do very well before taking the course cannot expect to show this kind of gain: Those who already are getting A's can hardly expect to do much better. Similarly, while any one technique may make a substantial difference in how much students learn, additional techniques necessarily yield smaller gains. If, for example, learning to network boosts a student's score from 65 percent to 91 percent, the maximum gain that can result from *all additional* training is obviously much smaller. What, then, is the effect of the entire program?

The first attempt to answer this question was made in 1977 (Dansereau, Collins, et al., 1979). That spring, students took the course using materials similar to those described above. They were compared to a group of students drawn from introductory psychology classes. Both groups of students studied typical textbook passages at the beginning, middle, and end of the semester, on which they were tested one week later. There was no difference between the two groups of students at the beginning of the semester, and there was still no difference at the midpoint. But at the end of the semester, those who had taken the Techniques course showed greater gains (compared to their original performance) than did those without training.

Dansereau and his colleagues thought the course might have had some general attitudinal benefits as well, so they had their students fill out questionnaires designed to find out about test anxiety, study habits, concentration problems, and feelings about academic competence. The results revealed greater positive changes on all measures among those who had taken Dansereau's course.

Although the results of the 1977 study were positive, some weaknesses in the course were revealed. The course materials were modified accordingly, and in the fall of 1978, Dansereau (Dansereau, et al., 1980) undertook a second study to assess the revised course. The experiment followed essentially the same plan as the previous study. As before, there was no difference in learning ability between trained and untrained students midway through the semester, but by the end of the course the Techniques students had a clear advantage on essay and short-answer questions.

Dansereau offers some evidence that the effects of training do not end with the semester. Three months after the 1978 study ended, Dansereau sent a ten-item questionnaire to the students who had taken his course. They indicated on a 0 to 8 scale (from no effect to extremely positive effect) what influence the course had had on such things as the ability to understand textbooks, efficiency in studying, and grades received. The ratings indicated that the students believed the course had had a "moderate to strong" positive effect on their lives as students.

The program is not, however, without its problems. The most important of these is the fact that the materials are not readily available. The course materials have not been published, and sample units are available only in mimeographed form.

A second problem is that the units do not form a tightly integrated set of materials. For instance, the first unit is on the MURDER metastrategy. The rest of the course is supposed to provide techniques for performing the steps in MURDER, but Dansereau is vague about how the techniques fit into the metastrategy. There also are a number of inconsistencies from one unit to the next. In one unit the students are advised to follow certain procedures in studying texts; in another, the advice is to follow a different set of procedures. Dansereau recognizes that these problems exist and recommends that educators consider each of the units independently. "We don't encourage people to adopt the entire course," he says. "Instead, we suggest that they look over the various units, select those that seem appropriate to their purposes, and use them."[14]

It would be easier to do just that if there were some sort of teacher's manual to accompany the units. The latter are intended to be largely self-instructional, and they may be, although in teaching the course Dansereau does more than hand out the ditto materials for each unit. But there is no teacher's manual, text, or article that describes how to go about administering the course.

Finally, those who adopt the course, or some adaptation of it, may encounter opposition to it from certain teachers. One college instructor objected in particular to the idea of teaching students to anticipate what questions a teacher might ask on a test. He even went so far as to say that if he found that a student of his earned an A on a test by having used such techniques, he would not hesitate to change the grade to F. While this reaction probably is exceptional, there is no doubt that there will be those who oppose efforts to teach some of the strategies offered in the course.

Despite these problems, the course has much to recommend it. The unit on mood-modifying techniques may help students who lack confidence in themselves. The unit on various knowledge schemas gives the student an orderly way of thinking about course content. The unit on networking provides step-by-step exercises that gradually build skill by way of a more sophisticated technique than outlining or note taking. As Dansereau himself says, the course is a kind of smorgasbord of learning techniques. Perhaps no one will be pleased with every dish, but almost everyone will find something on the menu palatable.

9   Thoughtful Teaching

In the programs described thus far, instruction in thinking is quite deliberately set off from the rest of the school day. Thinking is treated as a distinct subject, comparable to, but not dependent upon, standard courses. Teachers who conduct these thinking lessons encourage their students to apply what they learn to their regular subjects, but for the most part such carry-over is not built into the program, nor is it considered essential to its success. The assumption of these stand-alone programs is that thinking is best taught independently of traditional coursework. There is an alternative to this approach.

Assumptions and Goals

The alternative, which I will call thoughtful teaching, is to incorporate thinking into the curriculum, to teach thinking in the very process of teaching English, history, science, math, and every other subject. According to this view, we ought not to separate thinking from the rest of the curriculum; students ought to be learning and using thinking skills throughout the school day. This is not to say that advocates of thoughtful teaching are opposed to independent thinking programs. In fact, there is nothing inconsistent about incorporating thinking instruction into the standard curriculum while at the same time offering programs such as Philosophy for Children and CoRT Thinking Lessons. But those who advocate thoughtful teaching believe that whether special programs are offered or not, students should receive thinking instruction as part of their regular coursework.

The concept is not new.[1] There always have been teachers who considered thinking part of their subject matter. But the idea of incorporating thinking skills into the curriculum has received

THOUGHTFUL TEACHING

Principal developer: Numerous people, including classroom teachers, have developed various versions of thoughtful teaching. The present version is hypothetical.

Assumptions: Thinking is inseparable from content, so thinking is best taught in the context of standard course material.

Goals: To teach students to apply various thinking skills to their school assignments. Skills taught vary; the present version includes self-talk, imaging, paraphrasing, and other techniques.

Methods and materials: Methods vary. The present version uses modeling, prompting, and positive reinforcement. The materials are the text and other standard materials of the course.

Audience: Adaptable to any group. The present version probably is most suitable for upper-elementary and secondary-school students.

Teacher qualifications: Training is highly desirable. Some workshops are available in variations of this approach. Teachers must have a superior grasp of course content and the thinking skills taught.

Benefits claimed: Students acquire facility in the thinking skills taught and can apply them to academic tasks; improved mastery of course content.

Special problems: Lack of support (teacher's guide); some methods (including modeling, prompting, and reinforcing) involve subtleties of administration.

increasing support from psychologists in recent years. Robert Glaser (1984) of the University of Pittsburgh, for example, argues that thinking is not something that one learns in an abstract way and then applies to whatever situation comes along. Rather, learning to use a thinking skill inevitably means learning to use it in a particular context. The implication is that a student cannot learn, for example, "to solve problems"; instead, the student must learn to solve math problems, science problems, language problems, history problems, and so on. Similarly, one does not become skillful at critical thinking; one learns to think critically about politics, or science, or law, or whatever it is that one has been taught to think critically about. Thus, the more situations in which students learn to apply a thinking skill, the more situations in which they will be able to apply it. As a result, many experts agree with Canadian psychologist Carl Bereiter (1984) that "the promotion of thinking skills should be deeply embedded in the whole fabric of an instructional program" (p. 77).

There are, of course, hundreds of ways of going about embedding instruction in thinking into the curriculum. There may, in fact, be hundreds of such programs in use, many of them informally developed by classroom teachers. It probably is impossible to write a description of thoughtful teaching that would closely resemble what a majority of these programs offer students. What follows, then, is merely *one* version of this approach, a *hypothetical* program that I offer for illustrative purposes.

We may begin with the question, What thinking skills are to be taught? Of course, one of the advantages of thoughtful teaching is that the skills taught are not dictated in advance; the teacher may select any skill that seems suitable. One way to get ideas for such skills is to review formal thinking programs; another is to search the educational and psychological journals. Here is one possible list of skills:

SELF-TALK.   Many students do not talk to themselves as they read a story, recall information, or solve a problem, yet such covert speech can improve performance on these and other tasks.

IMAGING.   A strategy for enhancing understanding and recall is to imagine the relevant items. On hearing a talk on the composition of blood, for example, students might imagine themselves floating in the bloodstream and seeing corpuscles, platelets, and other objects as they are described by the teacher. These images might be conjured up later in an effort to recall the lecture.

PARAPHRASING.   Translating what one has read or heard into one's own words forces one to come to grips with it. When good students finish reading a passage, they often attempt to summarize what they have read; poor students can learn to do the same thing.

SEEKING ADDITIONAL INFORMATION.   Students sometimes fail to understand something because they have too little information. Frequently, they simply memorize the material. If they seek additional information, what once seemed arbitrary or mysterious makes sense and there is no need to memorize.

MNEMONICS.   When memorizing cannot be avoided, the student can invent various mnemonics to make the task easier: acronyms (NATO); abbreviations (DNA, RNA); acrostics (Every Good Boy Does Fine); rhymes (*i* before *e* . . .), and the like. (Note that the skill involves *inventing* mnemonics as the need rises, not merely making use of those provided by someone else.)

NETWORKING.   Organizing material into a kind of knowledge map that forces one to think about the relationships among the facts and ideas (see chapter 8) can enhance understanding and recall and can improve the use of information (in writing essays, for example).

GRAPHIC REPRESENTATION.   Figures, tables, diagrams, sketches, and the like are handy ways of representing information. They can simplify a complex set of facts, help students recall information, or point to the solution of a problem.

SIMPLIFYING.   One way of tackling a complex problem is to work on a simpler version of it. The student who cannot solve the problem $20/30 \times 12/24$ may find it helpful to try the problem $2/3 \times 1/2$.

DECOMPOSING.   Another way of dealing with a complex task is to divide it into small parts and then work on those parts. Writing a term paper consists, for example, of choosing a topic, reading, narrowing the topic, outlining, writing a first draft, and so on. A task that seems overwhelming often presents no problem when broken down in this way.

CHECKING.   Simply rereading a difficult passage, looking over one's work, or redoing a problem, perhaps in a different way, are easy ways of catching errors, inconsistencies, and other flaws.

Any number of other skills might be added to this list. Many teachers may want their students to know how to do a PMI (see chapter 2); some may want to teach students to express arguments in syllogisms; some may prefer outlining to networking; some may want to teach students to use schemas when studying (see chapter 8).

Methods and Materials

Teachers who decide to incorporate thinking instruction into regular coursework are also free to choose from a wide variety of teaching methods. Glaser (1984), for example, suggests teaching thinking through "interrogation and confrontation," by which he means the case study, discovery, and inquiry methods. However, in the hypothetical program under consideration here, thinking skills are to be taught by a three-pronged method consisting of modeling, prompting, and reinforcing. This approach relies heavily upon the work of Harvard psychologist B. F. Skinner (1968).

Modeling consists of demonstrating the skill to be learned. For example, two Canadian psychologists (Meichenbaum and Goodman, 1971) demonstrated the use of self-talk to elementary students by thinking aloud as they worked on a task that involved copying line patterns:

> Okay, what is it I have to do? I have to copy the picture with the different lines. I have to go slowly and carefully. Okay, draw the line down, down, good; and then to the right, that's it; now down some more and to the left. Good, I'm doing fine so far. Remember, go slowly. Now back up again. No, I was supposed to go down. That's okay. Just erase the line carefully . . . Good. Even if I make an error I can go on slowly and carefully. I have to go down now. Finished. I did it! (p. 117)

Self-talk also is useful when trying to recall information, and a teacher can demonstrate this by thinking aloud while struggling to recall a name. The effort might go something like this: "Let's see.

He's Italian. He's usually referred to by both the first and last name, as in "John Smith," but both his names have three or four syllables. The first starts with an *l* sound—Lee, Lester, Linus, Leroy, Leonard . . . Leonard, Leon-ard . . . Leonardo! That's it, Leonardo da Vinci!"

The same sort of process can be demonstrated while working science or mathematics problems before the class. Teachers have always worked such problems before their students, but these demonstrations typically fail to illustrate the false starts, dead ends, and other mistakes people typically make when working on problems. Thoughtful teachers, on the other hand, let the students "listen in" on their thoughts as they work so that students see not only how to solve the problem but how to detect and correct errors along the way.

Other thinking skills can be modeled in the same way. Teachers may model imaging by pausing to describe what they "see" while reading a poem or story.[2] Paraphrasing is easily demonstrated by stating the gist of a student comment or a passage in a text. Networking may be modeled by developing a network on the blackboard while talking about, say, the structure of American government. Note that the skills are not modeled in an abstract or hypothetical way removed from regular course content. Rather, the thinking skills are modeled in the process of teaching standard subject matter.

Modeling is important in teaching thinking skills for the same reason it is important in teaching athletic skills: It allows the student to see what the skill actually looks like. But while modeling provides something to imitate, it does not ensure imitation. For this reason, thoughtful teachers must prompt the use of the skills they have modeled.

The word *prompt* is a term that psychologists borrowed from the theater, and its meaning is much the same: Prompting means doing something to induce a person to perform some act (such as speaking the lines of a play). Thoughtful teachers prompt their students to use thinking skills in various ways.

The simplest and most direct kind of prompt consists of asking students to imitate some modeled thinking skill. Again, this is the same method that is used in teaching physical skills. The basketball coach shows his students how to shoot foul shots and then says,

"OK, now you try it." A classroom teacher does much the same thing when, having demonstrated self-talk while reading a story, he asks a student to read a story aloud and comment to the class while reading. Similarly, a student who cannot recall a person's name might be asked to talk to himself out loud as a way of dredging up the memory. And instead of merely having a student work out a math problem on the chalkboard, the teacher might ask her to think aloud as she works.

Other thinking skills may be prompted in the same direct manner. Students may be asked to imagine the scene depicted in a story that is being read, and the teacher may stop reading periodically to ask the students to describe the scenes they envisage. Likewise, a teacher can paraphrase one paragraph in an essay, then read the next paragraph and ask a student to paraphrase it. When it becomes clear that a student does not understand some concept or relationship, he might be asked to seek additional information. Students can be asked to think up mnemonics to help them remember some rule or fact, to simplify a problem or break it into parts, and so on.

Sometimes a single prompt of this sort is not enough. The student who makes no reply when asked to use self-talk as a way of recalling a name might be given hints—not about the name, but about the use of self-talk. The teacher might say, "Can you remember anything about the name? The letter it starts with, perhaps?" Similarly, students who, when asked to paraphrase an essay, simply repeat everything they can recall about it might be asked which of the recalled points are the most important; they might then be asked to summarize these points in one or two sentences.

Sometimes the teacher may have to use a series of prompts. For instance, the student who is unable to describe a scene depicted in a story may be asked specific questions about the text. The exchange might go something like this:

TEACHER: Where does the scene take place?
STUDENT: Outside.
TEACHER: Where outside? In the city? In the suburbs?
STUDENT: In the country.
TEACHER: How do you know it's in the country?
STUDENT: It talks about the sky, and the fresh air, and they're sitting under a big tree looking at a farm.

TEACHER: Close your eyes and see if you can see them sitting under the tree. Got it?

STUDENT: Yes.

TEACHER: OK. What does the tree look like? How big is it?

Once students are able to use a skill when asked, the next step is to teach them to use the skill without being asked. The goal of teaching thinking skills is to have students use the skills on their own when appropriate, and not merely when asked to do so. To help students reach this point, teachers should gradually fade out the use of prompts. This is done by going from explicit requests for the performance of a skill to strong hints that the skill should be used, then to weak hints, and finally to providing merely the opportunity for the use of the skill.

The pace of prompt fading is controlled by the students. Once students are quite capable of performing a skill on request, the teacher may shift from direct requests for its use to hints. For instance, instead of asking students to use diagrams, the teacher may ask, "How can we represent this problem on the board?" When students readily reply to such questions by suggesting the appropriate skill, it is time to move on to subtler hints, such as, "How can we make this problem clearer?" When students readily respond to such weak hints, the teacher should try presenting tasks without comment.

Even after students have reached the point of using a thinking skill without being prompted to do so, they will nevertheless sometimes fail to avail themselves of it. When this happens, the teacher should return to the use of prompts. However, in this event it is best to begin with the weakest prompts and move to stronger prompts only if the student fails to respond.

One very effective way of prompting a student to use a skill he seems to have forgotten is simply to wait a few seconds. As noted in chapter 1, many teachers give students only about a second to begin answering a question. This is hardly enough time to use the thinking skills that might help them. By increasing "wait-time," teachers give students the opportunity to use thinking skills, and it may be for this reason that increased wait-time is associated with longer, more relevant, and more sophisticated answers (Dillon, 1984; Gall, 1984). Even simple recall questions may provide the opportunity to use thinking skills if the teacher is willing to wait. Given time, the student who cannot immediately recall a fact might, through the use of self-talk, networking, or other skills, be able to come up with it. Ten seconds of silent waiting while a student talks to herself or draws diagrams can seem an eternity in a classroom, but we cannot hope that students will use thinking skills if they are not given the opportunity to do so.

Prompting skill use is a vital part of thoughtful teaching because students need to perform a thinking skill if they are to learn it. However, some people mistakenly believe that if students repeatedly perform a skill, they are assured of mastering it. Practice, they assume, makes perfect. But while practice may be necessary for the acquisition of a skill, it is not usually sufficient; reinforcement also is important.

Positive reinforcement, or what most people call reward, is the most powerful tool available to the teacher.[3] It is all too often neglected (see, for example, Sadker and Sadker, 1985). In fact, many teachers rely almost exclusively upon what psychologists call aversive control: punishment or the threat of punishment. Students are asked to study in order to avoid receiving a poor grade, having a note sent to their parents, being required to stand in the corner. Such tactics are widely used chiefly because they tend to be very effective in the short run: The noisy student who is shouted at or threatened with detention usually quiets down, at least temporarily. But positive reinforcers, particularly praise, smiles, eye contact, and the like, are more effective in the long run, especially when the object is to teach the student *to do* something rather than *not to do* something.[4] Thoughtful teaching requires the systematic reinforcement of the thinking skills being taught.

It is important to understand that reinforcement means that praise and the like are contingent upon the performance of the skill being learned. Some teachers assume that if a student produces the desired product (an answer or a problem solution), it is enough to reward that. But Skinner (1968) points out that this is *not* an effective way of teaching thinking. He likens this approach to teaching swimming by throwing children into a pool: Some will make it to the edge of the pool, with rewarding results, but it is a mistake to say that these children have been *taught* how to swim. To teach swimming, Skinner argues, the teacher must reinforce the specific skills that go into swimming. To teach thinking, the teacher must reinforce the specific skills that go into thinking. The focus must be the performance of the skill, not the product that results from the use of the skill.

It might be thought that "contrived" reinforcers (those that come from the teacher, as opposed to the thinking activity itself) should be unnecessary. Afterall, if the thinking skills taught are effective, the good results the skills produce will be their own reward, and a more powerful reward than any that might come from a teacher. Thinking skills do produce rewarding results, but often these natural reinforcers (succeeding at a task, solving a problem, recalling a fact, figuring something out) are ineffective because they are delayed and uncertain, especially during the early stages of learning. A student may tackle a difficult problem by first working a simpler version of it, but even so he may not reach the correct solution. Then, too, the skills themselves may seem at first to be awkward and a waste of time.[5] A student who routinely works on tasks in an impulsive, hit-or-miss fashion may feel foolish talking to himself about what he is doing. Networking can be helpful in a variety of learning situations, but it is apt to be confusing at first. Thus, in order to establish and maintain the use of thinking skills until the natural reinforcers become effective, it is necessary to use contrived reinforcers such as praise. Fortunately, such reinforcers are immensely effective.[6]

Of course, the student's first attempts at any new skill are apt to be clumsy, so it is unrealistic to praise only perfect performances. Instead, the thoughtful teacher reinforces improvement. Almost any attempt at, say, networking is praised at first. Then, as the students begin to improve upon these primitive efforts, the teacher reinforces only the better performances. In this way, the teacher slowly "raises the ante," gradually requiring more and more sophisticated performances for reinforcement until the skill is thoroughly mastered.[7]

When students begin to learn a skill, teachers should reinforce its use as often as possible. However, in an ordinary classroom situation, it is impractical, if not impossible, to reinforce the use of a thinking skill by every student. Fortunately, it is not necessary to do so. Any time a teacher publicly reinforces the use of a skill by one student, the use of that skill by others is vicariously reinforced. For instance, if Mary represents a complex theory in an elegant diagram on the chalkboard, her teacher might say, "Mary, that diagram really helps clarify the theory." If, in answering a question, a student breaks it down into three parts and then treats each part in turn, his teacher might say, "I liked the way you broke the question into parts, John." Such comments have their most powerful effect upon the students to whom they are directed, but they are not lost on the others in the class. While direct reinforcement is desirable, vicarious reinforcement is effective and practical (Bandura, 1977).

While students are learning a thinking skill, the frequency of reinforcement should remain high. Eventually, however, students must be weaned of teacher reinforcers in much the same way that they are weaned of teacher prompts. Only in this way will students become independent of the teacher and continue to use the skill on their own. Therefore, once the students have mastered a skill, the teacher should reduce the frequency of reinforcement. This does not mean, however, that when the students have learned to use mnemonics, say, that the teacher is through teaching mnemonics. Rather, the focus shifts from teaching students how to use the skill (which requires frequent reinforcement) to teaching students to use the skill (which requires infrequent reinforcement). This is accomplished by gradually increasing the number of times the skill is used between reinforcements.

This technique, which Skinner (1968) calls "stretching the ratio," is more difficult than it sounds. If teachers decrease the rate of reinforcement too quickly, the students may stop using the skill even though they know how to use it. If the teacher continues to reinforce at a high rate, skill use may remain teacher-dependent. The solution would seem to be to stretch the ratio until student use of a skill declines, then increase the rate of reinforcement slightly before "stretching" again.

One characteristic of thoughtful programs is that they teach thinking skills without benefit of special "thinking exercises." Standard classroom exercises serve for teaching both course content and thinking skills. However, certain kinds of class exercises may be more useful in teaching thinking than others, while nevertheless serving quite well for teaching course content. For instance, Raths and his colleagues (1967) suggest that teachers prepare a list of statements (about history, say, or science) and have the students determine which are facts and which are inferences. Another writer (Beyer, 1983) recommends asking students to say which of a series of statements subsumes the others.

Teachers sometimes can get ideas for thought-provoking exercises from the research literature. For example, some researchers (e.g., Markman, in press) have conducted experiments in which children read passages containing some sort of implicit contradiction. Other investigators (see Bransford, 1979) have used ambiguous passages to study how people detect gaps in their understanding. Teachers might use similar materials as a way of teaching students to represent ideas graphically, to paraphrase, or to check their work.

Certain kinds of group work can provide excellent opportunities for the use of thinking skills. Canadian psychologist Jacqueline Tetroe (reported in Scardamalia and Bereiter, in press) has found that a particularly thought-provoking activity involves giving a group of students a sentence and asking them to write a story that would conclude with that sentence. One such last sentence was, "So that is how Melissa came to be at a laundromat at midnight with one million dollars in her bag and a mob of angry people behind her." This assignment forces students to find ways to meet the constraints of the last sentence, and this requires some hard thinking. And we have seen (in chapter 7) that pair problem solving can be used to teach certain thinking skills. There is, then, no shortage of activities through which the teacher may teach both course content and thinking skills.

Target Audience

Since the present thoughtful-teaching program is hypothetical, we can only speculate about the audience for which it would be best suited. However, it seems safe to say that a program of this sort can be used with students in all grades and at virtually every ability level. The skills described above have been taught successfully to a wide range of students. And modeling, prompting, and reinforcing are thoroughly sound pedagogical techniques that have been used successfully with all sorts of students and all sorts of subject matter. Moreover, since the standard course materials for a given group of students also serve as thinking lessons, there is not much question about the suitability of the material. However, teachers undoubtedly will need to adapt the program to their particular students. In particular, the choice of skills to be taught, the rate at which they are introduced, the speed with which teachers fade prompts, the form and frequency of reinforcement—all will vary from one group of students to another. Nevertheless, it seems clear that the program has wide applicability.

Teacher Training and Qualifications

The matter of who should teach the program is less clear. All teachers model new skills, prompt students to perform them, and reinforce their correct use. But teaching thoughtfully probably requires a more sophisticated grasp of these skills than some teachers possess. The fading of prompts is not routinely taught in teacher education programs; many teachers use reinforcers far too sparingly to be effective in teaching new material; and the concept of "stretching the ratio" is completely unknown to many educators. Even reinforcing the use of skills is not as simple as it seems. More than one teacher has used reinforcement incorrectly and then concluded, "It doesn't work." Moreover, those who would teach students to use networking, say, must have mastered the skill themselves, yet it may be as new to some teachers as it is to those they are teaching. Clearly, then, some sort of training would seem highly desirable. There is as yet no training available in the particular brand of thoughtful teaching described here, but there are people who offer workshops on ways of embedding thinking into the standard curriculum.[8]

Evaluation

Assuming that the teacher feels comfortable about attempting thoughtful teaching, what advantages may he or she expect over traditional teaching? First, there is no doubt that the model–prompt–reinforce method, properly used, is effective. And numerous studies have demonstrated that, with such instruction, students readily learn imaging, networking, mnemonics, paraphrasing, and other thinking skills. In the study by Meichenbaum and Goodman (1971), cited earlier, children not only learned self-talk and used it appropriately when asked to, but in a one-month follow-up most of the children were observed talking to themselves spontaneously while working on a problem. In another study (Levin, 1973), fourth graders learned to image while they read. In other studies, high school students greatly improved their recall of facts by learning to use mnemonics (see Bower, 1973). The value of teaching the thinking skills proposed here is clearly demonstrated. But what about the entire program?

There are, of course, no studies of the hypothetical form of thoughtful teaching described here. However, there is at least one study that may be instructive. In the public schools of Marion, Indiana, an attempt was made to teach mathematics in a new way (Wheatley, 1983/1984). The new approach involved a number of changes, but the researchers believe that the key element was a shift in emphasis from rule memorization to a more thoughtful approach. Teachers taught elementary students to solve problems using thinking skills such as drawing diagrams and breaking problems into parts. The students then worked in small groups to solve math problems using these strategies. Each year the students took the Iowa Test of Basic Skills, a standardized achievement test frequently used in elementary schools. The test showed a sharp rise in math achievement: Students who had scored at the 28th percentile in grade three (before the new program) scored at the 82nd percentile three years later. Moreover, the students improved in simple computation skills as well as mathematical problem solving.

It is worth repeating that the Marion study is not a test of the thoughtful-teaching program described here. But Marion's success in mathematics means that it is reasonable to suppose that teaching thinking skills in conjunction with writing, history, science, literature, and other subjects can improve both thinking *and* the mastery of traditional content.

There may be other benefits. The emphasis on student use of thinking skills means that the student becomes an active participant, not a passive observer, in school learning. And since what the student is asked to think about is school subjects, those subjects really are "food for thought." With thoughtful teaching, therefore, school may become a more interesting and challenging place for the student.

It may become more interesting and challenging for the teacher, as well. For the traditional teacher, the goal is to cover the material in the curriculum guide, the same material the teacher may have covered a dozen times before. This can get as tiresome for the teacher as it is for the student. With thoughtful teaching, on the other hand, the focus of the lesson is thinking. The teacher's goal is to improve the student's ability to *act upon*, not merely absorb, the information in the curriculum. And since students can find an infinite number of ways of acting upon information, teachers are less likely to get bored.

It must be admitted, however, that these likely benefits have yet to be documented in any rigorous way. For although the idea of incorporating thinking skills into the curriculum has been around a long time, it is just beginning to receive serious attention. Moreover, like every other thinking program reviewed here, thoughtful teaching is likely to bring with it problems as well as benefits.

The most obvious problems with the version of thoughtful teaching described here stem from the fact that it is a hypothetical program. This means that there is no teacher's guide and no formal training program. Teachers can learn about the intricacies of modeling, prompting, and reinforcing from various educational and psychological textbooks, but they are not likely to find much on how these techniques can be used to teach thinking skills in the process of teaching ordinary coursework. Unfortunately, the same problem will confront teachers who use many other versions of thoughtful teaching.

One problem with any form of thoughtful teaching is that it probably requires superior mastery of course content. It is one thing to teach the standard material in a curriculum guide; it is quite another thing to teach students to apply thinking skills to that material. If a student paraphrases an essay, creates a table, or represents data in diagrams, it can hardly be expected that he will go about it in exactly the same way as the teacher might. The teacher may have to know the subject very well in order to understand what the student is attempting to do.

A third problem teachers may encounter is resistance from students. Thoughtful teaching runs counter to what many students have come to think of as education. Older students, in particular, may have become so accustomed to performing school tasks *without* thinking that they may resist any effort to change their long-standing habits. The student who habitually guesses when she does not immediately recall the correct answer may not appreciate the teacher's efforts to get her to use self-talk. She will certainly be right in believing that the teacher's way is more work, and it may be no easy task to convince her that the effort is worthwhile.

Finally, thoughtful teaching has the disadvantage of being invisible. That is, there is no separate thinking lesson, no special booklets, few buzzwords to bandy about. Thoughtful teaching does not have a lot of special "bells and whistles" that parents and other school visitors can be shown as proof that "we're teaching thinking." Although this may seem a superficial matter, the lack of visibility inherent in thoughtful teaching may make it difficult to generate support for the program. Even teachers may be inclined to yawn and say, "I already do that."

Of course, anyone familiar with traditional teaching who spends half an hour in a thoughtful teacher's class will recognize that something very special is going on, something very different from what most teachers "already do." In traditional teaching, the student is a passive recipient of revealed wisdom, handed down by the teacher; in thoughtful teaching, the student is an active "knowledge worker" whose task is to grasp, manipulate, and use information. Thoughtful teaching may not give education a shiny new look, but it offers a profound change in what education is all about.

10 Conclusion

The preceding chapters were intended to give the reader a brief introduction to each of several approaches to the problem of teaching thinking. These chapters necessarily focused upon the ways in which the programs differ from one another. It might be helpful at this point to consider some of the ways in which they are alike. The following are ten points upon which most, if not all, of the foregoing program developers agree.

1. **Thinking is a skill and can be taught.** Many people view thinking as a natural ability that develops without instruction. But those who set out to teach thinking assume that it is at least partly a learned skill. Some people who quarrel with this view ask, "If thinking is learned, why are some people so much better at it than others?" Arthur Whimbey (1975; see chapter 7) responds to this question with another question: "Well, why are some adults good swimmers whereas others flounder and sink? Why are there good athletes—gymnasts, football players, expert equestrians— whose swimming might be described as optimistic splashing?" (p. 120). Of course, there may be many reasons for such differences. But, as Whimbey notes, "an instructional method that regards swimming as a pattern of skills can make almost anyone a competent swimmer" (p. 120). In the same way, if we view thinking as a set of skills, we may find ways of teaching those skills so that almost anyone can become a competent thinker. This isn't to say that "raw talent" isn't important. Training in any skill necessarily builds upon a foundation of genetic endowment, and differences in endowment will affect how a student profits from training.[1] The point is that, with proper instruction, nearly all students will improve their ability to think.

2. **Thinking is best taught by direct and systematic instruction.** Many people assume that if thinking is learned, it

is learned in the course of ordinary experiences at home and at
school and does not require special instruction. It is true that reading, writing, solving math problems, and other tasks improve thinking ability. It is also true that walking, running, and playing help
youngsters acquire skills useful in gymnastics, but no one thinks
that expertise at gymnastics is the automatic by-product of such
activities. To master gymnastics skills, the student must receive
formal training in those skills. To master thinking skills, the student
must receive formal instruction in those skills. The program developers agree that the best way to teach thinking is with a head-on
approach.

3.   **The emphasis of instruction in thinking should be upon
the process of thinking, not its products.**   Most of education
focuses upon the "right answers" to questions. Those who teach
thinking make their focus the steps that go into producing answers,
rather than the answers themselves. Thus, whether a student answers
correctly or not, these teachers want to know how the student
arrived at the answer.

4.   **Students must use the thinking skills they are to
learn.**   No skill is learned entirely by the lecture method. We may
tell a student how to swim the backstroke, but that, in itself, does
not enable him to perform adequately in the water. Similarly, students do not learn how to think merely by hearing lectures about
thinking skills; they must use those skills themselves. Training in
thinking must, therefore, provide ample opportunity to practice the
skills being studied. This may take the form of workbook-type
exercises, but it should also include frequent verbal exchanges
between the teacher and the students and among the students.
Guided practice is far more effective than mere repetition, so most
of the practice should be done under the watchful eye of a skillful
teacher.

5.   **Teachers should reinforce the appropriate use of
thinking skills.**   Most program developers recommend that
teachers praise (or otherwise reinforce) students when they make
valid inferences, suggest interesting ideas, use suitable strategies,

and so on. The appropriate use of thinking skills should be reinforced throughout the school day, not merely during thinking lessons.

6. Teachers should make allowances for individual and developmental differences among students. Students differ both in how they think and in how they learn, and such differences should be taken into account when administering any program. Sometimes this means deleting certain activities, providing additional activities, teaching different students in different ways, or modifying the program materials.

7. Thinking should be taught in a relaxed, nonthreatening atmosphere. Toward this end, thinking activities should not be graded; cooperation should be encouraged and competition minimized; and students should be encouraged to take time to think before answering questions. Teachers should correct thinking errors (faulty logic, the misuse of strategies, and the like), but they should do so in a nonpunitive way.

8. Thinking must be taught over a period of years. It takes years of training and practice to become a skillful gymnast or pianist. Thinking is at least as complex as these skills and requires the same sort of prolonged and intense study. We ought not to teach thinking in the fifth grade, say, and then forget about it. Although some of the programs reviewed here are intended to take a year or less to administer, it probably is safe to say that all the program developers believe that thinking instruction should not end with the last lesson in a program. The students might begin another program, or the teacher might continue to reinforce the use of skills learned earlier.

9. An effort must be made to see that the skills taught in the program carry over to other subjects. No program author is satisfied to have students think well during the thinking lessons but poorly at other times. The point is to have students use their new skills throughout the school day and outside the school as well. Teachers can encourage such generalization by calling upon students to use their skills in other settings and by praising good thinking wherever it occurs.

10.   The teacher is the single most important determinant of the success of a thinking program.   This follows from several of the points just made: It is the teacher who reinforces skill use, who encourages students to use the skills, who establishes the class climate, who provides for individual differences, who encourages skill transfer, and so on. Not everyone can teach thinking effectively. Most program developers believe that to be effective, teachers must have certain skills and attitudes. They must, for example, be competent at the thinking skills they will teach. And a teacher who lacks enthusiasm for a program and conveys those negative feelings to the students will practically ensure its defeat.

Whether the reader intends to adopt one or more of the programs described, look elsewhere for another program, or design a new thinking program, it would be a good idea to refer now and then to the above points of agreement. But regardless of how one proceeds to teach thinking, there are certain general pitfalls that must be avoided. Program developers generally have little to say about these common hazards. Let us consider ten of the more important ones.

1.   Moving too fast.   It is easy to become so enthusiastic about a new movement that we jump in without having first laid the proper groundwork. Before embarking upon any thinking program, teachers and school administrators would do well to review the key questions identified in chapter 1: What assumptions underlie the program? What are its goals? How does it attempt to teach thinking? What is the target audience? What special characteristics or training will its teachers require? What benefits can be expected? And what special problems will there be? If any of these questions cannot be answered to the satisfaction of those involved (including the teachers who will administer the program), it is probably a mistake to implement the program.

2.   Doing too much.   It is easy to make lists of fifty, a hundred, or even more skills students might learn. As Harvard's Jerome Bruner (in press) points out, the danger in attempting to teach long lists of skills is that there may be so much ground to cover that the focus will shift from teaching the process of thinking to teaching a body of facts about thinking. Students then end up learning to describe good thinking, rather than learning to think well.

3. **Expecting too much.** One problem with any innovation is that it tends to be viewed as a cure for all ills. All too often we come to expect that a change in curriculum, scheduling, or teaching method will raise SAT scores, end vandalism, improve attendance, fire up burned-out teachers, eradicate drug abuse, and maybe even make the teacher's lounge a little larger. Sometimes the spokespersons for thinking-skills programs encourage unrealistic expectations by exaggerating the benefits that can be expected.[2] Claims for anything more than modest success should be discounted: It is better to have modest expectations exceeded than to be disappointed.

4. **Taking the short view.** George Bonham (reported in Sadler, 1982), editor of *Change Magazine*, has said that one thing that all educational innovations have in common is brevity of duration. Although it is commonly thought that this is because the innovations do not pan out, the fact is that even highly successful programs are often discarded. Most experts would probably agree that if a thinking-skills program is to be implemented, it should be done with a view toward keeping it (barring evidence of catastrophic results) for a minimum of three years. This also will help to keep expenses down.

5. **Neglecting evaluation.** Evaluation often is thought of as something to be done later, but plans for evaluation should be made before a program is implemented. This is good advice even in the case of an individual teacher who decides to teach thinking on his or her own, but it is certainly wise when an entire school or school district will be using a program. The evaluation probably should focus upon criterion-referenced tests (tests especially designed to measure facility in the skills the program attempts to teach). Other useful measures of success may include ratings by independent observers of student essays and class discussions, ratings by parents, and self-ratings by students. There is no harm in determining whether a program has improved academic achievement, but it must be remembered that scores on standardized achievement

tests depend a great deal upon the mastery of certain facts, not just upon thinking ability. (Studying thinking in the eighth grade will not teach the student the math or history he should have learned in the seventh grade.)

6. **Neglecting the home environment.**   Numerous authors (deAvila and Duncan, in press; Franklin, in press; Simmons, in press) have suggested that the child's home environment has a powerful impact upon the development of thinking. Jerome Bruner (in press) notes that many middle-class parents have a "hidden agenda" that includes teaching their children to be reflective, to think things through, to use their heads. A good deal is known about the role parents play in the development of thinking abilities, but none of the programs described earlier, nor any other that I know of, makes full use of this knowledge. Yet we need not assume that educational programs must stop at the schoolhouse door. A school that succeeds in changing parental behavior, even in small ways, might greatly enhance the effects of its thinking program.

7. **Becoming satisfied.**   Regardless of what program is adopted or how successful it may be, it ought not to be considered the final word on the subject. Teachers and administrators should keep an eye out for new developments, experiment with new techniques from time to time, and write to the program developers to request help with recurring problems. No thinking program is ever really finished.

8. **Waiting for something better.**   Even though the programs now available are not perfect, it is a mistake to postpone efforts to teach thinking. For one thing, our students cannot wait. Each day that passes without instruction in thinking is one less day in which to improve thinking. For another thing, there is much to learn from attempting to teach thinking. Edward deBono (1976) puts it this way: "No matter how imperfect it may be, something that is actually in use can tell us more about the teaching of thinking than any amount of theory or 'test-tube' experimentation" (p. 230).

9. **Neglecting traditional course material.**   Thinking, important as it is, is not the only thing students must learn in

school. Yale psychologist Robert Sternberg (in press), who is developing a thinking-skills program of his own, writes that "on the one hand, I do not think schools have done enough to train children how to think. . . . On the other hand, our [schools] . . . will not be improved if one kind of excess is replaced with another."

10. Giving in to early failures. Canadian psychologist Donald Meichenbaum, who teaches thinking skills to children with learning problems, recommends that we take a clinical approach to teaching thinking. When a doctor's first efforts to help a patient are not successful, he does not conclude that the problem is untreatable; he modifies the treatment and tries again. Meichenbaum (in press) suggests that we take the same view in teaching thinking: If the first efforts are disappointing, modify the treatment and push on. Too many educational programs are scrapped prematurely with the explanation, "We tried that. It didn't work."

As this last point implies, mistakes are inevitable. We are, after all, just beginning. And there are many questions that no one can yet answer: Which skills are the most important to teach? What skills should be taught at a given grade? How rapidly should skills be introduced? How much practice is enough? What is the best way to make the use of thinking skills habitual? What is the best way to encourage transfer of the skills to regular coursework?

Despite the problems and the unanswered questions, we must make a beginning. We must commit ourselves to the goal of teaching students how to think. If our first efforts fail, we must try again, and then again and again. After all, what alternative do we have? A new world is in the making, a world that requires thoughtful, intelligent people. The movement to put thinking in our schools is basic if today's youth are to meet the challenges of that new world.

Epilogue

The reader of this short introduction to thinking programs might well ask at this point, "What next? Where do I go from here?" The answer depends upon where "here" is.

Readers who are enthusiastic about one of the programs described might begin by rereading the relevant chapter in this book, including the notes. They will then want to move on to a study of the course materials and supporting literature (teacher's manual and so forth) for that program. Next they may read books and articles about the program. (The most important of these are provided in the reference list.)

Readers who want to explore other programs should spend some time in the educational-materials section of a good library. Another way to find programs is to find out what various schools are doing. Many school districts have developed or are developing their own thinking programs, and may be willing to share materials and ideas.

Those readers who want to design their own programs would be well advised to take advantage of the published literature on the subject. Certain professional journals in psychology and education sometimes carry articles relevant to thinking instruction. Two periodicals that are particularly likely to run articles of practical use are *Educational Leadership* and *Phi Delta Kappan*. In 1984, *Educational Leadership* devoted the September and November issues to thinking instruction; anyone seriously interested in designing a program will want to study both of these issues carefully. Newsletters that may also prove helpful include *Teaching Thinking & Problem Solving* (Lawrence Erlbaum Associates) and *Human Intelligence* (P.O. Box 1163, Birmingham, Michigan 48012).

Workshops, conferences, and institutes on teaching thinking are being offered around the country. Many of these are announced in periodicals such as *The Chronicle of Higher Education, Educational Leadership,* and *Problem Solving.* School districts and professional organizations may want to invite experts to give talks or lead workshops. Teachers also may find it helpful to learn more about thinking skills by taking thinking courses. An alternative is to read "how to" books on thinking such as Polya's *How to Solve It*, Hayes's *The Complete Problem Solver*, and Bransford and Stein's *The IDEAL Problem Solver*.

The Association for Supervision and Curriculum Development has initiated a thinking-skills network to aid communication among those of its members who are interested in thinking instruction. Readers who are not members of ASCD but are interested in the network should write to Ronald Brandt, ASCD, 225 N. Washington St., Alexandria, Virginia 22314.

Those who want to study the more technical aspects of thinking and thinking instruction should see the two-volume work, *Thinking and Learning Skills*, edited by Judith Segal and associates (1985) and Susan Chipman and associates (in press). These books are collections of papers written by psychologists and other specialists. They are aimed more at researchers than at teachers and school administrators, but they contain much useful material. I had manuscript versions of these books while writing and have cited them frequently. Two other technical books in this area are *Thinking: The Expanding Frontier* (Maxwell, 1983) and *Teaching Thinking* (Nickerson, Perkins, and Smith, in press). The latter book was unavailable as of this writing, but prepublication publicity suggests that it provides a detailed treatment of research on thinking skills and their instruction.

NOTES
REFERENCES
INDEX

Notes

Chapter 1. Introduction

1. Brandt, R., personal communication, March 1, 1985.

2. Two goals, both involving thinking, tied for first place: (1) to develop the ability to think—creatively, objectively, analytically; (2) to develop good work habits, the ability to organize one's thoughts, the ability to concentrate.

3. The thinking movement is not, however, an exclusively American phenomenon. Interest in thinking is strong in many nations. In 1979, Venezuela established the Ministry for the Development of Human Intelligence, a cabinet-level post whose director is charged with developing ways of improving the thinking skills of the nation's schoolchildren (Dominquez, 1985; Walsh, 1981).

4. One problem with this argument not examined here is that poor student thinking is not new. Bloom and Broder (1950) and Holt (1964) reported the same kinds of deficiencies seen today in the "good old days" of the 1950s.

5. I have not attempted to answer the question of per pupil cost, since this depends on the number of students involved, the length of time the program is continued, and many other variables.

Chapter 2. CoRT Thinking Lessons

1. This anecdote is drawn from deBono (1976; 1985).

2. DeBono expounds upon his theories about thinking at length in various publications, but see especially deBono (1969; 1976; 1985).

3. For more on the pattern-making brain, see deBono (1976). What deBono is talking about is remarkably similar to what psychologists call perceptual sets. A perceptual set is defined as a predisposition to perceive a situation in a particular way. In the nine-dots problem, for example, the task is to draw four straight lines through a three-by-three array of dots without lifting the pencil from the paper. (If the problem is new to you, try solving it before reading further.) The difficulty of the problem lies in the fact that people ordinarily see the dots as a square within which the pencil lines must stay. To solve the problem, it is necessary to break

this perceptual set. It would appear that deBono is attempting to teach students to break or avoid such sets.

4. Nevertheless, deBono (1984) asserts that critical thinking ("second stage thinking") is important, and is taught in CoRT through lessons on evidence, analysis, and the like.

5. DeBono is quite adamant on this point. He writes that "long philosophical discussions, even if they do finally resolve the matter, leave too great a residue of confusion. *Make it a rule to emphasize what is clear, and avoid what is doubtful*" (deBono, 1975, p. 21 of *CoRT III Teacher's Notes*; emphasis added). Elsewhere deBono (1976) writes that "it is better for the teacher to be confident and wrong than hesitant and right" (p. 172). DeBono's opposition to what he calls "the danger of philosophizing" (1976, p. 176) puts him at odds with some other program developers, most notably Matthew Lipman (see chapter 4).

6. DeBono (1976) insists that "the ideas that turn up are not important. What is important is the thinking process that is practiced in turning up ideas" (p. 145).

7. In contrast, most other program developers strongly urge teachers to review skills covered earlier. In fact, some build review into their programs. See particularly the Productive Thinking Program (chapter 3).

8. For the most part, deBono claims only that the program changes behavior. But he suggests (deBono, 1985) that it is "just conceivable" that practice in thinking may have a chemical effect upon the brain. A similar idea is advanced by Feuerstein regarding Instrumental Enrichment (see chapter 6, note 11).

9. Presumably, what Polson and Jeffries have in mind is that studies typically involve asking students to generate ideas on some topic, rather than giving them some sort of carefully prepared test. DeBono (1976) responds that "it must seem a convenient policy to reject the use of standardized tests that might show the ineffectualness of thinking courses," but he adds that "you do not measure a person's honesty by measuring his height" (p. 202).

10. DeBono, E., personal communication, May 29, 1985.

Chapter 3. Productive Thinking Program

1. Note the difference between this view and that of deBono (chapter 2).

2. The programmed feature means, of course, that the lessons must be taken in sequence. Students must not be allowed to skip a lesson; students who miss lessons because of absences must make up those lessons before going on.

3. As this language suggests, the program attempts to incorporate methods drawn from discovery learning and inquiry training, as well as programmed instruction.

4. Again, note the difference between this view and that of deBono (chapter 2). Review is an important part of the Productive Thinking Program, while deBono discourages it.

5. This is one way in which the program attempts to get students to "transfer" their learning to regular schoolwork. Such transfer attempts are not always built into thinking programs.

6. See Polson and Jeffries (1985) for their comments on the program's value.

7. See Polson and Jeffries (1985) for more on this.

8. Covington, M. V., personal communication, April 4, 1985.

Chapter 4. Philosophy for Children

1. Lipman, M., personal communication, April 3, 1982.

2. Ibid. This is very different from the view underlying the thoughtful-teaching approach (chapter 9).

3. Thirty of these skills are discussed in Lipman (1985). Yale psychologist Robert Sternberg (1984), whose special area of research is the identification of the thinking skills that make up intelligent behavior, writes that the skills taught in Philosophy for Children "are clearly the right ones to teach for both academic and everyday information processing . . . " (p. 44).

4. Lipman, M., personal communication, April 3, 1982. The name Harry Stottlemeier is a play on the name of Aristotle.

5. These techniques are described at length in Lipman et al. (1980) and in Lipman (1985).

6. In this, Lipman resembles deBono (chapter 2).

7. In this, Lipman is in sharp disagreement with deBono (chapter 2); see especially note 5 of that chapter.

8. One teacher (Minkowitz, 1979) writes of an eleven-year-old boy who could not read at all, yet participated intelligently in a discussion on the ethics of eating animals.

9. Qualities required of teachers are discussed in Lipman et al. (1980) and Lipman (1984).

10. For more numbers, see Appendix B of Lipman et al. (1980); Cinquino (1980); and the various studies reported in *Thinking, the Journal of Philosophy for Children.* Also see the reviews by Bransford et al. (1985) and Sternberg (1984).

11. See Goldman (1984) on the "dangers" of teaching philosophy. In a reply to Goldman, Paul (1984) asks, "Is there in the case of Philosophy for Children any tangible evidence to indicate that its version of the socratic method unnerves, disorients, or otherwise adversely affects children in the least? I contend that the evidence is all in the opposite direction—that children are encouraged by it, develop more self-confidence, come to think of learning and dialogue as fruitful, and view truth as not less but *more* within their personal grasp" (p. 63f).

Chapter 5. Odyssey

1. Like Philosophy for Children (chapter 4), Odyssey claims to teach both analytical thinking and creative thinking. However, the emphasis in both clearly is on reasoning. This contrasts with the CoRT program (chapter 2) and, to a lesser extent, the Productive Thinking Program (chapter 3), both of which emphasize creative thinking.

2. Although dialogue is important, there does not seem to be much interest

in open discussion in the sense striven for in the Philosophy for Children program (chapter 4); in Odyssey the goal seems to be to have the students interact with the teacher, rather than with each other.

3. In this, the program resembles Philosophy for Children (chapter 4) and Problem Solving and Comprehension (chapter 7), and contrasts with CoRT Thinking (chapter 2), in which the teacher remains firmly in charge.

4. Nickerson, R., personal communication, November 2, 1984.

Chapter 6. Instrumental Enrichment

1. Feuerstein, R., personal communication, July 28, 1981.

2. Sternberg (1984) claims that Instrumental Enrichment probably "has been the most widely used and field-tested program, both in this country and abroad" (p. 42).

3. Feuerstein contends that standard IQ tests measure past learning, not learning potential. He therefore designed an instrument, the *Learning Potential Assessment Device* (Feuerstein, 1979a), to measure learning ability through a test-teach-test procedure. For a very brief introduction to the LPAD, see Chance (1981).

4. Feuerstein (personal communication, July 28, 1981) adds that "any attempt to really change a person must involve a reorientation—a total reorientation—of his encounters with reality. He must be turned from a passive observer of the world who merely reproduces what he sees and hears, to a person who acts on the world, transforming it to his purpose." In extreme cases, Feuerstein believes, this may mean removing the child from the home environment. In this, he is supported by Clarke and Clarke (1976).

5. The program is sometimes called Feuerstein's Instrumental Enrichment, or FIE. The program materials are published under the title *Just a minute . . . Let me think* (Feuerstein, 1978). The teacher's guide is by Feuerstein and Hoffman (1980). The theory on which the program is based is discussed in Feuerstein (1977, 1980) and in Feuerstein, Jensen, Hoffman, and Rand (1985).

6. This is the problem of transfer. See chapter 3, note 5.

7. Feuerstein, R., personal communication, July 28, 1981.

8. In this, the program contrasts sharply with the Productive Thinking Program (chapter 3), which is said to work well without teacher involvement. Like Philosophy for Children (see chapter 4), Instrumental Enrichment is teacher-dependent.

9. In Israel, Instrumental Enrichment is often merely part of a global therapeutic effort that may include medical treatment, psychotherapy, foster care, and carefully arranged social activities. In addition, the program is administered individually in severe cases, and sometimes a student goes through the entire course two or more times. It is impossible to generalize from such experience to ordinary classroom use of the program.

10. Feuerstein disputes this (personal communication, April 11, 1985).

11. Feuerstein (1979b) believes that Instrumental Enrichment changes

behavior, but he also raises the possibility that the program produces organic changes in the brain. (Compare this with deBono; see chapter 2, note 8.)

12. Feuerstein, R., personal communication, July 28, 1981. It should be noted, however, that the same criticism (an initial loss of efficiency) probably applies to other thinking programs.

Chapter 7. Problem Solving and Comprehension

1. Whimbey, A., personal communication, June 14, 1982.

2. Ibid.

3. Ibid.

4. See Whimbey and Lochhead (1982) for more on these traits. Also see Whimbey (1975). His views are nicely summarized in Whimbey (1976; 1984).

5. Sometimes the model solutions take the form of think-aloud protocols of expert problem solvers, and sometimes they take the form of summary statements of the steps essential for solution. Solutions to the additional practice items are included in the teacher's guide.

6. See Lochhead (1985) for more on the teacher's role.

7. Lochhead, J., personal communication, May 24, 1982. Compare this comment with Feuerstein's on the delayed effects of Instrumental Enrichment (chapter 6, note 12).

8. Carmichael, J. W., personal communication, June 16, 1982. Also see Carmichael (1979); Carmichael, et al. (1979; 1980); and Whimbey, et al. (1980).

9. Whimbey and Lochhead (1982) say that students can expect to spend between ten and forty hours on the program, depending upon how many problems they attempt to solve.

Chapter 8. Techniques of Learning

1. Dansereau, D. F., personal communication, July 21, 1982.

2. Ibid.

3. Ibid.

4. For reviews of this research, see Dansereau (1978; 1985) and Dansereau, Actkinson, Long, and McDonald, (1974).

5. Dansereau's program is offered as a course at Texas Christian University under the name of Techniques of College Learning. But since the program is not synonymous with the course (under a different instructor the *course* might be quite different) and is not exclusively aimed at college students, I have called the program Techniques of Learning. The program is similar to that of Claire Weinstein (1978; Weinstein and Underwood, 1985); for a comparison of the two programs, see Campione and Armbruster (1985). Readers also may want to examine the Learning to Learn program of Marcia Heiman (1980).

6. Dansereau, D. F., personal communication, July 21, 1982.

7. Dansereau's program has not been published; the version described here consists of numerous mimeographed booklets, most dated 1978. Yet Dansereau has indicated that the program has been further revised (personal communication, March 22, 1985).

8. This peer modeling seems similar to Whimbey's pair learning (chapter 7).

9. Dansereau's MURDER is reminiscent of Robinson's (1961) SQ3R study method, but Dansereau (1985) says that whereas Robinson merely told students what to do, he (Dansereau) provides training in what to do.

10. Although this unit was originally to appear at this point in the program, Dansereau now presents it last. He reports (1985) that students seem to gain more from the program when the mood strategies are taken up last.

11. For more on networking, see Holley, Dansereau, McDonald, Garland, and Collins (1979), or Dansereau and Holley (1981).

12. Dansereau, D. F., personal communication, July 21, 1982.

13. Ibid.

14. Ibid. Dansereau reports that recent revisions in the program have corrected some of the problems reviewed here (personal communication, March 22, 1985).

Chapter 9. Thoughtful Teaching

1. Raths, Wasserman, Jonas, and Rothstein (1967) and others proposed something along these lines called "teaching for thinking" in the 1960s. Much also has been written about the benefits of discovery teaching (e.g., Shulman and Keisler, 1966) and inquiry training (e.g., Collins and Stevens, 1982). What does seem to be new is the idea of making specific thinking skills (such as those taught by independent programs) part of the curriculum.

2. See Collins and Smith (1980) for more on modeling various thinking skills during reading.

3. Positive reinforcement refers to the procedure of strengthening (that is, increasing the likelihood of) some behavior by following the behavior with a reinforcer (smiles, praise, and the like). The correct use of reinforcement is more difficult than many people realize. The teacher who tells his noisy students, "Be quiet and I'll let you go to recess early," gets the quiet he desires, but he has reinforced noisiness, not quietness, since it was noisiness that produced the promise. He has therefore increased the likelihood that the children will be noisy in the future—especially just before recess. For more on this, see Skinner (1968).

4. Skinner (1968) argues cogently for a change from the aversive measures so much in evidence to the use of positive reinforcement.

5. This is a problem noted by Dansereau as well (chapter 8).

6. This discussion of contrived and natural reinforcers follows Skinner (1968).

7. For more on this process, called shaping, see Skinner (1968) or Alberto and Troutman (1982).

8. Barry Beyer (George Mason University) and Art Costa (California State University at Sacramento) are among those who have given workshops on their own approaches to thoughtful teaching. In addition, ASCD is developing a video-based in-service program on teaching thinking. A film, *Improving the Quality of Student Thinking*, also is available from the association.

Chapter 10. Conclusion

1. It is a mistake to assume that teaching thinking to all students, however effectively, will erase the differences in thinking among them. If we tested the swimming abilities of a hundred randomly selected healthy youngsters, we would find wide differences. If we then gave these youngsters the best swimming instruction possible, all of them would improve, but the gap between those at the head of the class and those at the bottom would not disappear. (It might, in fact, widen.) The point, however, is that all of the students would be more skillful swimmers. It is a mistake to think that education can eradicate differences among students. But education can bring out the best in each student. For more on this point, see Hunt (1961).

2. For instance, one program author said that since students using his program for about fifty hours had gained an average of one hundred points (one standard deviation) on an aptitude test, students might show gains of three hundred points if they were to train for three hundred hours. This *might* be true, but there is no basis for such an extrapolation. I could give many examples of such exaggerated, or at least unsubstantiated, claims.

References

Alberto, P., & Troutman, A. (1982). *Applied Behavior Analysis for Teachers*. Columbus, OH: Charles E. Merrill.

Arbitman-Smith, R., Haywood, H. C., & Bransford, J. D. (1978). Assessing cognitive change. In C. M. McCauley, R. Sperber, & P. Brooks (Eds.), *Learning and cognition in the mentally retarded*. Baltimore, MD: University Park Press.

Bandura, A. (1977). *Social learning theory*. Englewood Cliffs, NJ: Prentice-Hall.

Bereiter, C. (1984). How to keep thinking skills from going the way of all frills. *Educational Leadership, 42*(1), 75–77.

Bettelheim, B., & Zelan, K. (1982). *On learning to read*. New York: Knopf.

Beyer, B. K. (1983). Common sense about teaching thinking skills. *Educational Leadership, 41*(13), 44–49.

Bloom, B. S., & Broder, L. J. (1950). *Problem-solving processes of college students*. Chicago: University of Chicago Press.

Bower, G. H. (1973). Educational applications of mnemonic devices. In K. O. Doyle (Ed.), *Interactions: Readings in human psychology*. Boston: D. C. Heath.

Bransford, J. D. (1979). *Human cognition: Learning, understanding and remembering*. Belmont, CA: Wadsworth Publishing Co.

Bransford, J. D., Arbitman-Smith, R., Stein, B. S., & Vye, N. J. (1985). Improving thinking and learning skills: An analysis of three approaches. In J. W. Segal, S. F. Chipman, & R. Glaser (Eds.), *Thinking and learning skills, Vol. 1: Relating instruction to research* (pp. 133–208). Hillsdale, NJ: Lawrence Erlbaum Associates.

Bransford, J. D., & Stein, B. (1984). *The IDEAL problem solver*. San Francisco, CA: Freeman.

Brandt, R. (1984). Learning about thinking. *Educational Leadership, 42*(3), 3.

Brent, F. (1979). Philosophy in the middle-school student, part 2. *Thinking, the Journal for Philosophy for Children, 1*(2), 39.

Brown, A. L., & Smiley, S. S. (1977). Rating the importance of structural units of prose passages: A problem of metacognitive development. *Child Development, 48*, 1–8.

Bruner, J. (in press). On teaching thinking: An afterthought. In S. F. Chipman, J. W. Segal, & R. Glaser (Eds.), *Thinking and learning skills, Vol. 2: Research and open questions*. Hillsdale, NJ: Lawrence Erlbaum Associates.

Burnes, B. (1982). Harry Stottlemeier's Discovery—the Minnesota experience. *Thinking, the Journal for Philosophy for Children, 3*(1), 8–11.

Campione, J. C., & Armbruster, B. B. (1985). Acquiring information from texts:

An analysis of four approaches. In J. W. Segal, S. F. Chipman, & R. Glaser (Eds.), *Thinking and learning skills, Vol. 1: Relating instruction to research* (pp. 317–362). Hillsdale, NJ: Lawrence Erlbaum Associates.

Carmichael, J. W. (1979). Cognitive skills-oriented PSI in general college chemistry. Mimeograph: Department of Chemistry, Xavier University of New Orleans.

Carmichael, J. W., Hassell, J., Hunter, J., Jones, L., Ryan, M. A., & Vincent, H. (1980). Project SOAR (stress on analytical reasoning). *The American Biology Teacher, 42,* 169–173.

Carmichael, J. W., Ryan, M. A., & Whimbey, A. (1979). Cognitive skills oriented PSI. *Journal of Developmental and Remedial Education, 3,* 4–6.

Chance, P. (1981, October). The remedial thinker. *Psychology Today,* pp. 63–73.

Children discuss degrees and kinds of difference. (1979). *Thinking, the Journal of Philosophy for Children, 1*(1), 58–70.

Chipman, S. F., Segal, J. W., & Glaser, R. (Eds.). (in press). *Thinking and learning skills, Vol. 2: Research and open questions.* Hillsdale, NJ: Lawrence Erlbaum Associates.

Cinquino, D. (1980). *Evaluation of the philosophy for children program.* Unpublished manuscript submitted to Glen Rock (NJ) Board of Education.

Clarke, A. M., & Clarke, A. D. (1976). *Early experience: Myth and evidence.* New York: Free Press.

Collins, A., & Smith, E. E. (1980). *Teaching the process of reading comprehension* (BBN Technical Report No. 4393). Cambridge, MA: Bolt Beranek and Newman.

Collins, A., & Stevens, A. L. (1982). Goals and strategies of inquiry teachers. In R. Glaser (Ed.), *Advances in instructional psychology, Vol. 2* (pp. 65–119). Hillsdale, NJ: Lawrence Erlbaum Associates.

Covington, M. V. (1985). Strategic thinking and the fear of failure. In J. W. Segal, S. F. Chipman, & R. Glaser (Eds.), *Thinking and learning skills, Vol. 1: Relating instruction to research* (pp. 389–416). Hillsdale, NJ: Lawrence Erlbaum Associates.

Covington, M. V., Crutchfield, R. S., Davies, L., & Olton, Jr., R. M. (1974). *The productive thinking program: A course in learning to think.* Columbus, OH: Charles E. Merrill.

Crutchfield, R. S. (1965). Instructing the individual in creative thinking. In Educational Testing Service, *New approaches to individualizing instruction* (pp. 13–26). Princeton, NJ: Educational Testing Service.

Dansereau, D. F. (1978a). The development of a learning strategy curriculum. In H. F. O'Neil, Jr. (Ed.), *Learning strategies* (pp. 1–30). New York: Academic Press.

Dansereau, D. F. (1978b). *Increasing concentration and motivation: Programmed text exercises #1.* Unpublished manuscript, Texas Christian University, Forth Worth.

Dansereau, D. F. (1978c). *Test taking hints.* Unpublished manuscript, Texas Christian University, Forth Worth.

Dansereau, D. F. (1978d). *Understanding and memorizing: The first step in test taking.* Unpublished manuscript, Texas Christian University, Forth Worth.

Dansereau, D. F. (1985). Learning strategies research. In J. W. Segal, S. F. Chipman, & R. Glaser (Eds.), *Thinking and learning skills, Vol. 1: Relating instruction to research* (pp. 209–240). Hillsdale, NJ: Lawrence Erlbaum Associates.

Dansereau, D. F., Actkinson, T. R., Long, G. L., & McDonald, B. (1974). *Learning strategies: A review and synthesis of the current literature* (AFHRL-TR-74-70). Lowry Air Force Base, CO: Technical Training Division.

Dansereau, D. F., Collins, K. W., McDonald, B. A., Holley, C. D., Garland, J., Diekhoff, G., & Evans, S. H. (1979). Development and evaluation of a learning strategy training program. *Journal of Educational Psychology, 71*(1), 64–73.

Dansereau, D. F., & Holley, C. D. (1981, September). *Development and evaluation of a text mapping strategy.* Paper presented to International Symposium on Text Processing. Fribourg, Switzerland.

Dansereau, D. F., Holley, C. D., Collins, K. W., Brooks, L. W., McDonald, B., & Larson, D. (1980). *Validity of learning strategies/skills training* (AFHRL-TR-79). Lowry Air Force Base, CO: Technical Training Division.

Dansereau, D. F., McDonald, B. A., Collins, K. W., Garland, J., Holley, C. D., Dickhoff, G. M., & Evans, S. H. (1979). Evaluation of a learning strategy system. In H. F. O'Neil, Jr., & C. D. Spielberger (Eds.), *Cognitive and affective learning strategies* (pp. 3–43). New York: Academic Press.

De Avila, E. A., & Duncan, S. (in press). The language-minority child: A psychological, linguistic and social analysis. In S. F. Chipman, J. W. Segal, & R. Glaser (Eds.), *Thinking and learning skills, Vol. 2: Research and open questions.* Hillsdale, NJ: Lawrence Erlbaum Associates.

deBono, E. (1969). *The mechanism of mind.* New York: Simon and Schuster.

deBono, E. (1975). *CoRT Thinking.* London: Direct Educational Services. (Now published by Pergamon Press.)

deBono, E. (1976). *Teaching thinking.* London: Maurice Temple Smith.

deBono, E. (1984). Critical thinking is not enough. *Educational Leadership, 42*(1), 16–17.

deBono, E. (1985). The CoRT Thinking program. In J. W. Segal, S. F. Chipman, & R. Glaser (Eds.), *Thinking and learning skills, Vol. 1: Relating instruction to research* (pp. 363–388). Hillsdale, NJ: Lawrence Erlbaum Associates.

Dillon, J. T. (1984). Research on questioning and discussion. *Educational Leadership, 42*(3), 50–56.

Dominguez, J. (1985). The development of human intelligence: The Venezuelan case. In J. W. Segal, S. F. Chipman, & R. Glaser (Eds.), *Thinking and learning skills, Vol. 1: Relating instruction to research* (pp. 529–536). Hillsdale, NJ: Lawrence Erlbaum Associates.

Durkin, D. (1978). *What classroom observations reveal about reading comprehension instruction* (Tech. Rep. No. 106). Urbana-Champaign: University of Illinois, Center for the Study of Reading.

Falkof, L., & Moss, J. (1984). When teachers tackle thinking skills. *Educational Leadership, 42*(3), 4–9.

Feuerstein, R. (1977). Mediated learning experience: A theoretical basis for cognitive modifiability during adolescence. In P. Mittler (Ed.), *Research to practice in mental retardation, Vol. 2: Education and training* (pp. 105–116). Baltimore, MD: University Park Press.

Feuerstein, R. (1978). *Just a minute . . . Let me think.* Baltimore, MD: University Park Press.

Feuerstein, R. (1979a). *The dynamic assessment of retarded performers: The learning potential assessment device, theory, instruments and techniques.* Baltimore, MD: University Park Press.

Feuerstein, R. (1979b). Ontogeny of learning. In M. Brazier (Ed.), *Brain mechanisms in memory and learning.* New York: Raven Press.

Feuerstein, R. (1980). *Instrumental enrichment: An intervention program for cognitive modifiability.* Baltimore, MD: University Park Press.

Feuerstein, R., & Hoffman, M. B. (1980). *Teacher's guide to the Feuerstein Instrumental Enrichment program.* Baltimore, MD: University Park Press.

Feuerstein, R., & Jensen, M. R. (1980, May). Instrumental Enrichment: Theoretical basis, goals and instruments. *Education Forum,* pp. 401–423.

Feuerstein, R., Jensen, M., Hoffman, M. B., & Rand, Y. (1985). Instrumental Enrichment, an intervention program for structural cognitive modifiability: Theory and practice. In J. W. Segal, S. F. Chipman, & R. Glaser (Eds.), *Thinking and learning skills, Vol. 1: Relating instruction to research* (pp. 43–82). Hillsdale, NJ: Lawrence Erlbaum Associates.

Feuerstein, R., & Rand, Y. (1977). *Studies in cognitive modifiability. Instrumental Enrichment: Redevelopment of cognitive functions of retarded early adolescents.* Jerusalem: Hadassah-Wizo-Canada Research Institute.

Fletcher, M. A. (1984, October 16). New goal: Teaching Johnny how to think. *Evening Sun* (Baltimore), pp. C1, C2.

Franklin, A. J. (in press). The social context and socialization variables as factors in thinking and learning. In S. F. Chipman, J. W. Segal, & R. Glaser (Eds.), *Thinking and learning skills, Vol. 2: Research and open questions.* Hillsdale, NJ: Lawrence Erlbaum Associates.

Gall, M. (1984). Synthesis of research on teachers' questioning. *Educational Leadership, 42,*(3), 40–47.

Gallup, A. (1985). The Gallup poll of teachers' attitudes toward the public schools, part 2. *Phi Delta Kappan, 66*(5), 323–330.

Gisi, L. G., & Forbes, R. H. (1982). *The information society: Are high school graduates ready?* Denver, CO: Education Commission of the States.

Glaser, R. (1984). Education and thinking: The role of knowledge. *American Psychologist, 39*(1), 93–104.

Goldman, L. (1984). Warning: The Socratic method can be dangerous. *Educational Leadership, 42*(1), 57–62.

Goodlad, J. L. (1983). *A place called school.* New York: McGraw-Hill.

Graduates may lack tomorrow's "basics." (1982, fall). *NAEP Newsletter,* p. 8.

Haas, H. J. (1976). *Philosophical thinking in the elementary schools: An evaluation of the educational program Philosophy for Children.* Unpublished manuscript, Rutgers University, Institute for Cognitive Studies, New Jersey.

Harvard University, Bolt Beranek and Newman, Inc., & the Ministry of Education of the Republic of Venezuela. (in press). *Odyssey: A curriculum for thinking (Foundations of reasoning; Understanding language; Verbal reasoning; Problem solving; Decision making; Inventive thinking).* Watertown, MA: Mastery Education Corporation.

Hayes, J. R. (1981). *The complete problem solver.* Philadelphia, PA: Franklin Institute Press.

Heiman, M. (1980). *Learning skills instructor's manual.* Cambridge, MA: Learning Skills Consultants.

Herrnstein, R. J., Nickerson, R. S., de Sanchez, M., & Swets, J. A., (No Date). *Teaching Thinking Skills.* Unpublished manuscript.

Holley, C. D., Dansereau, D. F., McDonald, B. A., Garland, J. C., & Collins, K. W. (1979). Evaluation of a hierarchical mapping technique as an aid to prose processing. *Contemporary Educational Psychology, 4,* 227–237.

Holt, J. (1964/1970). *How children fail.* New York: Dell Publishing.

Hunt, J. M. (1961). *Intelligence and experience.* New York: John Wiley.

Hutchinson, R. T. (1985). Teaching problem solving to developmental adults: A pilot project. In J. W. Segal, S. F. Chipman, & R. Glaser (Eds.), *Thinking and learning skills, Vol. 1: Relating instruction to research* (pp. 499–514). Hillsdale, NJ: Lawrence Erlbaum Associates.

Levin, J. R. (1973). Inducing comprehension in poor readers: A test of a recent model. *Journal of Educational Psychology, 65,* 19–24.

Lipman, M. (1977). *Harry Stottlemeier's Discovery* (rev. ed.). Upper Montclair, NJ: Institute for the Advancement of Philosophy for Children.

Lipman, M. (1978). *Suki.* Upper Montclair, NJ: Institute for the Advancement of Philosophy for Children.

Lipman, M. (1979). *Mark.* Upper Montclair, NJ: Institute for the Advancement of Philosophy for Children.

Lipman, M. (1981). *Pixie.* Upper Montclair, NJ: Institute for the Advancement of Philosophy for Children.

Lipman, M. (1982a). *Kio and Gus.* Upper Montclair, NJ: Institute for the Advancement of Philosophy for Children.

Lipman, M. (1982b). Philosophy for Children. *Thinking, the Journal of Philosophy for Children. 3*(3,4), 35–44.

Lipman, M. (1983). *Lisa* (2nd ed.). Upper Montclair, NJ: Institute for the Advancement of Philosophy for Children.

Lipman, M. (1984). The cultivation of reasoning through philosophy. *Educational Leadership, 42*(1), 51–56.

Lipman, M. (1985). Thinking skills fostered by Philosophy for Children. In J. W. Segal, S. F. Chipman, & R. Glaser (Eds.), *Thinking and learning skills, Vol. 1: Relating instruction to research* (pp. 83–108). Hillsdale, NJ: Lawrence Erlbaum Associates.

Lipman, M., & Sharp, A. M. (1979). Some educational presuppositions of Philosophy for Children. *Thinking, the Journal of Philosophy for Children, 1*(2), 47–50.

Lipman, M., Sharp, A. M., & Oscanyan, F. S. (1979). *Philosophical inquiry: An instructional manual to accompany Harry Stottlemeier's Discovery* (2nd ed.). Upper Montclair, NJ: Institute for the Advancement of Philosophy for Children.

Lipman, M., Sharp, A. M., & Oscanyan, F. S. (1980). *Philosophy in the classroom* (2nd ed.). Philadelphia, PA: Temple University Press.

Lochhead, J. (1985). Teaching analytical reasoning skills through pair problem solving. In J. W. Segal, S. F. Chipman, & R. Glaser (Eds.), *Thinking and learning skills, Vol. 1: Relating instruction to research* (pp. 109–132). Hillsdale, NJ: Lawrence Erlbaum Associates.

Markman, E. M. (in press). Comprehension monitoring: Developmental and educational issues. In S. F. Chipman, J. W. Segal, & R. Glaser (Eds.), *Thinking and learning skills, Vol. 2: Research and open questions*. Hillsdale, NJ: Lawrence Erlbaum Associates.

Maxwell, E. (Ed.). (1983). *Thinking: The expanding frontier*. Philadelphia: Franklin Institute Press, 1983.

Meichenbaum, D. (in press). Teaching thinking: A cognitive-behavioral perspective. In S. F. Chipman, J. W. Segal, & R. Glaser (Eds.), *Thinking and learning skills, Vol. 2: Research and open questions*. Hillsdale, NJ: Lawrence Erlbaum Associates.

Meichenbaum, D., & Goodman, J. (1971). Training impulsive children to talk to themselves: A means of developing self-control. *Journal of Abnormal Psychology, 77*, 115–126.

Minkowitz, M. (1979). Discussion of rights at Police Athletic League. *Thinking, the Journal of Philosophy for Children, 1*(2), 54–56.

Morgenstern, C. F., & Renner, J. W. (1984). Measuring thinking with standardized science tests. *Journal of Research in Science Teaching, 21*(6), 639–648.

Naisbitt, J. (1982). *Megatrends: Ten new directions transforming our lives*. New York: Warner Books.

National Assessment of Educational Progress. (1980). *Writing achievement, 1969–79: Results from the third national writing assessment. Vol. 1: 17-year-olds* (Report 10-W-01). Denver, CO: Education Commission of the States.

National Assessment of Educational Progress. (1981). *Reading, thinking and writing: The results from the 1979–80 national assessment of reading and literature* (Report 11-L-01). Denver, CO: Education Commission of the States.

National Assessment of Educational Progress. (1983). *The third national mathematics assessment: Results, trends and issues* (Report 13-MA-01). Princeton, NJ: Educational Testing Service.

Nickerson, R. S., & Adams, M. J. (1983). Introduction. In *Project Intelligence: The development of procedures to enhance thinking skills, teacher's manual*. Cambridge, MA: Harvard University & Bolt Beranek and Newman, Inc.

Nickerson, R. S., Perkins, D. N., & Smith, E. E. (in press). *Teaching thinking*. Hillsdale, NJ: Lawrence Erlbaum Associates.

Olton, R. M., & Crutchfield, R. S. (1969). Developing the skills of productive thinking. In P. Mussen, J. Langer, & M. V. Covington (Eds.), *Trends and issues in developmental psychology* (pp. 68–91). New York: Holt, Rinehart and Winston.

Paul, R. W. (1984). The Socratic spirit: An answer to Louis Goldman. *Educational Leadership, 42*(1), 63–64.

Polson, P. G., & Jeffries, R. (1985). Instruction in general problem-solving skills: An analysis of four approaches. In J. W. Segal, S. F. Chipman, & R. Glaser

(Eds.), *Thinking and learning skills, Vol. 1: Relating instruction to research* (pp. 417–455). Hillsdale, NJ: Lawrence Erlbaum Associates.

Polya, G. (1957). *How to solve it*. Garden City, NY: Doubleday.

Project Intelligence: The development of procedures to enhance thinking skills, Final report. (1983). Cambridge, MA: Harvard University; Bolt Beranek and Newman, Inc.

Radford, J., & Burton, A. (1974). *Thinking: Its nature and development*. New York: John Wiley.

Raths, L. E., Wasserman, S., Jonas, A., & Rothstein, A. M. (1967). *Teaching for thinking: Theory and application*. Columbus, OH: Charles E. Merrill.

Reed, R., & Henderson, A. (1982). Analytical thinking for children in Fort Worth elementary schools: Initial evaluation report, summer, 1981. *Thinking, the Journal of Philosophy for Children, 3*(2), 27–30.

Robinson, F. P. (1961). *Effective study* (rev. ed.). New York: Harper and Brothers.

Roddy, J., & Watras, J. (1979). Challenging children to think. *Thinking, the Journal of Philosophy for Children, 1*(1), 5–9.

Rowe, M. B. (1974). Wait-time and rewards as instructional variables, their influence on language, logic and fate control. Part 1: Wait-time. *Journal of Research in Science Teaching, 11*, 81–94.

Sadker, D., & Sadker, M. (1985). Is the OK classroom OK? *Phi Delta Kappan, 66*(5), 358–361.

Sadler, W. A., Jr. (1982). A model for general education: Building a freshman core program based on cognitive skills. *Journal of Learning Skills, 1*(2), 35–40.

Sadler, W. A., Jr., & Whimbey, A. (1980, fall). Teaching cognitive skills: An objective for higher education. *National Forum*, 43–46.

Scardamalia, M., & Bereiter, C. (in press). Fostering the development of self-regulation in children's knowledge processing. In S. F. Chipman, J. W. Segal, & R. Glaser (Eds.), *Thinking and learning skills, Vol. 2: Research and open questions*. Hillsdale, NJ: Lawrence Erlbaum Associates.

Segal, J. W., Chipman, S. F., & Glaser, R. (Eds.). (1985). *Thinking and learning skills, Vol. 1: Relating instruction to research*. Hillsdale, NJ: Lawrence Erlbaum Associates.

Shulman, L. S., & Keisler, E. R. (Eds.). (1966). Learning by discovery: A critical appraisal. New York: Rand McNally.

Simmons, W. (in press). Social class and ethnic differences in cognition: A cultural practice perspective. In S. F. Chipman, J. W. Segal, & R. Glaser (Eds.), *Thinking and learning skills, Vol. 2: Research and open questions*. Hillsdale, NJ: Lawrence Erlbaum Associates.

Sirotnik, K. A. (1981). What you see is what you get: A summary of observations in over 1,000 elementary and secondary classrooms. *A study of schooling in the U.S.* (Technical Report Series No. 29). Los Angeles, CA: UCLA School of Education.

Sirotnik, K. A. (1983). What you see is what you get—consistency, persistency and mediocrity in classrooms. *Harvard Educational Review, 53*, 16–31.

Skinner, B. F. (1968). *The technology of teaching*. Englewood Cliffs, NJ: Prentice-Hall.

Sternberg, R. J. (1984). How can we teach intelligence? *Educational Leadership,* *42*(1), 38–48.

Sternberg, R. J. (in press). Instrumental and componential approaches to the nature and training of intelligence. In S. F. Chipman, J. W. Segal, & R. Glaser (Eds.), *Thinking and learning skills, Vol. 2: Research and open questions.* Hillsdale, NJ: Lawrence Erlbaum Associates.

Toffler, A. (1980). *The third wave.* New York: William Morrow.

Walsh, J. (1981). Plenipotentiary for Human Development. *Science, 214,* 640–641.

Weinstein, C. E. (1978). Elaborative skills as learning strategy. In H. F. O'Neil, Jr. (Ed.), *Learning strategies* (pp. 31–56). New York: Academic Press.

Weinstein, C. E., & Underwood, V. L. (1985). Learning strategies: The *how* of learning. In J. W. Segal, S. F. Chipman, & R. Glaser (Eds.), *Thinking and learning skills, Vol. 1: Relating instruction to research* (pp. 241–258). Hillsdale, NJ: Lawrence Erlbaum Associates.

Wheatley, G. H. (1983/1984). Problem Solving Makes Math Scores Soar. *Educational Leadership, 42*(4), 52–53.

Whimbey, A. (1975). *Intelligence can be taught.* New York: Dutton.

Whimbey, A. (1976, January). You can learn to raise your IQ score. *Psychology Today,* pp. 27–29; 84–85.

Whimbey, A. (1984). The key to higher order thinking is precise processing. *Educational Leadership, 42*(1), 66–70.

Whimbey, A., Carmichael, Jr., J. W., Jones, L. W., Hunter, J. T., & Vincent, J. A. (1980). Teaching critical reading and analytical reasoning in Project SOAR. *Journal of Reading, 24,* 5–10.

Whimbey, A., & Lochhead, J. (1982). *Problem solving and comprehension* (3rd ed.). Philadelphia: Franklin Institute Press.

Yang, P. M. (1979). Teaching philosophy to children in Taiwan. *Thinking, the Journal of Philosophy for Children, 1*(3&4), 10–13.

Index

161